Shorefishing

John Holden

Shorefishing

FABER & FABER
LONDON AND BOSTON

In the same series

COMPETITIVE JUDO
by George Glass

RALLYING
by Chris Sclater &
Martin Holmes

TABLE TENNIS
by Harold Myers

WATERSKIING
by Paul Seaton &
David Emery

SOCCER REFEREEING
by Jack Taylor

JUNIOR SOCCER
by John Jarman

First published in 1979 by
Faber and Faber Limited
3 Queen Square, London WC1N 3AU
Printed and bound in Great Britain by
Cox and Wyman Limited,
London, Fakenham and Reading
All rights reserved

© *John Holden 1979*

British Library Cataloguing Publication Data

Holden, John
  Shorefishing.
  1. Saltwater fishing
  I. Title
  799.1'2   SH57
  ISBN 0-571-11321-4
  ISBN 0-571-11389-3   Pbk

Contents

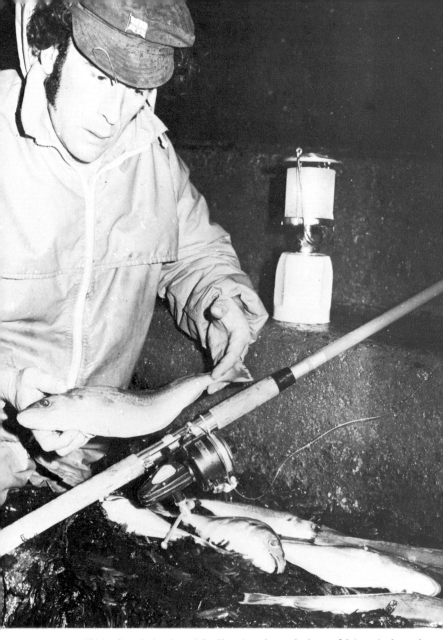

1 *Whiting from the beach at night. Knowing when and where to fish is again the result of observation and understanding of the ways of sea creatures.*

Introduction

The marine world is close-knit and secretive. If you wish to gather baits and go fishing, all very well; but you should not expect the sea and its creatures to co-operate. Every sign that eventually leads to success—gulls hunting along the surfline, marine animals washed up after a storm, or mackerel attacking a shoal of sandeels—is part of a jigsaw puzzle. Piecing it together creates a picture of life under the waves and might suggest a plan whereby the angler can outwit his quarry.

Angling is a recreation, but it is still the hunting of wild creatures and therefore governed by the laws of Nature, not the rules of man. To catch fish is to respond to deep, subconscious feelings. Perhaps true expertise is determined by the individual angler's genetic make-up; perhaps to differing degrees and for various reasons we are driven by the same hunting instinct that drew cavemen to the waterside.

Hair lines and bone hooks, the need to catch fish in order to survive—in short, bare necessity—have no place in angling. But the fact remains that regardless of sophisticated tackle, fishing is still man's interference in an alien world. Nature sets the pace, and the secret of fishing—if there really is a secret formula that can be learnt, rather than that which comes naturally—is close observation of natural history.

For those reasons alone, no fishing book can possibly teach anyone precisely how to catch fish. You have to learn for yourself in this game: get out there on the beach, look at the tidal and weather patterns, explore the tidepools, and, generally, try to tune in to the harmonies and rhythms of the seashore. All that can only be achieved by experience, and the apprenticeship is long and demanding.

But you cannot build angling skills on weak foundations. The most frequent trouble for anglers is that the basic mechanics of the sport hold back their progress. They cannot concentrate on the finer points of the sport because their tackle is poorly assembled, because their knots come undone too easily, because they lack the correct baits. Tackle and the methods of using it are a minor part of fishing, merely tools for our convenience and enjoyment, but they cause tremendous problems. If you are a beginner, how can you expect to learn about fishes and their world if every moment you spend on the beach is a nightmare of tangled lines?   This book, therefore, does not attempt to explain the art of angling. It is simply a practical guide to fishing methods: selecting tackle, tying knots, sharpening hooks and casting . . . all the things that have to be mastered in order to place a baited hook under the fish's nose. Everything is tried and tested and draws on not only the writer's experience of fishing and casting at British and international competition level, but also on the invaluable advice of the many expert anglers it is his good fortune to know.

2 *A big thornback ray caught in shallows. To outwit his quarry, the angler exploited the fish's preference for shallow, warm seawater close inshore, and its attraction to the oils drifting from fresh herring bait.*

1 *Shorefishing rods*

Beachcasting rods have always been surrounded by controversy: how long they should be, which action, how much sinker weight they ought to cast. Arguments have raged for years during which the market has been flooded with first one design then another. Battered by experts' opinion and seduced by manufacturers' advertisements, the average angler is utterly confused. Many change rods as each new one appears, in the hope of finding a design that will transform their casting and hook more fish. The perfect rod will never exist; it cannot, because every angler is different. Fishermen may be tall or short, weak or strong, athletic or arthritic. There are pendulum casts and South African casts and layback casts. Beaches may be flat and spacious, others steep and slippery, backed by cliffs. Each demands a different kind of rod.

Rod designing for other branches of angling is easier because tackle is used primarily for fishing. On the seashore, the ability to cast is essential, and casting performance of the rod matters a great deal. Shorecasting rods are therefore a compromise between casting and fishing, but unfortunately the tendency is to concentrate on casting so that the rod becomes difficult to use either for retrieving tackle or for fighting fish.

The rod must cast well, and in order for it to do so you may have to accept an inferior performance in other fields. That is inescapable. But the problem today is that many designers seem to have forgotten all about the rod's other tasks. If it were impossible to cast far enough with ordinary fishing tackle, special casting rods would be more acceptable. But nearly all rods cast well enough to satisfy the general demands of the sport.

I do not dispute that tournament rods cast farther. Special rods increase my own maximum distances from 175 to 230 yds (160 to 210m), but I would hate to fish with them because of their weight and poor balance. Long, powerful rods are fine for the extra distance, but useless when there is a big fish on the end of the line. The arguments for and against the use of specialised rods may be of interest to anglers but are of practical value to few. Unless you need to cast tremendous distances, stick to light, flexible *fishing* rods. By all means study the experts' methods, but do not follow them blindly.

ROD LENGTH

The most effective fishing tool is the handline. A strong line is sensitive and powerful enough to kill a big fish in a tenth of the time it would take to play on rod and reel. The mechanical inefficiency of the rod interferes with the pressure an angler imposes on a fish and favours the power and speed of the fish itself. The fish seems to fight harder, and the angler is restricted by the weakening effect of the rod's leverage. Every increase in rod length benefits the fish.

3 An 11ft (3·4 m), medium-fast action casting rod with a short handle is suitable for a great deal of British shorefishing with sinkers between 3 and 6 oz (85 and 170 g) and where huge fish are not expected. It is better if the rod is light enough to be held all day, because sometimes it is impractical to use a rod rest.

Sportsfishermen do not use handlines because they fish for enjoyment. The inefficiency of rods heightens sensations, and as long as the angler retains ultimate control, it is better if the fish can show its full paces. It is very important to make even small fish fight well, for most of the time that is all we catch. Planned, controlled weakness makes fishing more fun.

Fishes up to 30 lb (14 kg) may be handled easily on rods of about 9 ft (2.75 m) effective length (effective rod length is the distance in a straight line from rod tip to butt when the rod is fully flexed). In medium-fast action, the overall length of such a rod would be around 10–10½ ft (3–3.2 m). It helps to have the reel mounted as low as possible, right on the butt if you can learn to control it with the down-rod hand. If not, keep the handle as short as is consistent with good casting.

Rod length may be increased for fish of less than 15 lb (7 kg), with handle length correspondingly greater too. Rods up to 11½ ft (3.5 m) overall sacrifice only a small amount of fighting power, but the longer the rod, the longer the handle should be. The limiting factor for casting is the angler's shoulder width. Handles longer than shoulder width reduce casting because arms and shoulders cannot apply full strength.

ROD ACTION AND POWER

A rod is either powerful enough or it is not. Too much power is material wasted and weight added; rods that are too weak cave in under pressure. The only valid test is to cast and fish with the rod: if it copes with sinker weight and has just a hint of reserve power, it is fine. But there is a thin dividing line between reasonable insurance against breakage and excessive power, which will induce severe handling problems. Lightweight rods appeal to some anglers who boast of their prowess with weak tackle. You have to remember that light tackle is all

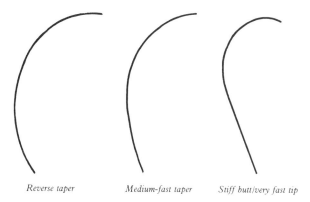

Reverse taper   *Medium-fast taper*   *Stiff butt/very fast tip*

Fig 1   Rod blank action

very well until you happen to hook a very big fish. It is too late then to wish for something stronger.

Theoretically, a specific rod action might be superior for a particular task: a very fast action casts a greater range of sinker weights than a slow taper does. In shorefishing practice, there is little to choose between actions, and the ultimate decision is of minor consequence. If the rod is of correct length and power, its action is largely a matter of personal preference: some anglers hate slow rods, others cannot cast well with very fast ones. On the tournament courts, fast-taper, stiff-butted rods of 15 ft (4.6 m) cast farthest, but their success does not imply that ordinary beach rods should imitate the design. Standard medium-fast blanks of either plain or compound taper are excellent for fishing.

General fishing with sinkers of 2–4 oz (55–155 g) demands a rod between 10 and 12 ft (3 and 3.7 m) long, perhaps a little longer for really light work. The rod must be light and comfortable because in many types of fishing it is necessary to hold the tackle all day. Heavy legering with 5–8 oz (140–225 g) sinkers needs a more powerful rod which, contrary to belief, should be shorter. Few anglers have the strength to use 6 oz (170 g) of lead and a 13 ft (4.0 m) rod. Although it will be used in a rod rest most of the time, there is still no excuse for massive weight in the heavier rod: a properly made beachcaster need be no more than 24 oz (680 g). A third very useful type of rod is the spinner. It will be used for lure and floatfishing with 2 oz (55 g) maximum sinker weight. Length can be as short as 8 ft (2.4 m), but for all-round versatility 10 ft (3 m) is better and especially useful for floatfishing where there are inshore obstructions that foul the line.

SHOREFISHING ROD CONSTRUCTION

Most modern rods are of moderate to fast taper with compound construction—the blanks are built up at certain spots along their length to improve action. A few rods still have the old reverse tapers, where the butt flexes under pressure. The action is said to help iron out overruns, but the price is a considerable loss of distance. Nevertheless, a reverse taper rod is most pleasant to fish with, and has far more feel to it than have many of the fast models.

A single-piece rod longer than 8 ft (2.4 m) is an embarrassment, so most rods are cut into two sections and joined by spigots or ferrules. The relative merits of the jointing methods are not worth arguing about; correctly made and fitted, either is perfectly good. The only clear advantage of the spigot is less tendency to stick and corrode.

Sometimes it is impractical to mould a full-length blank and the rod is made up by splicing or spigoting a length of parallel-wall glass or high-tensile duralumin to the butt. Duralumin is extremely stiff and improves the leverage, so that slightly better casting performance is achieved; but it ruins the feel of some blanks and may be too harsh for fishing. A disadvantage of the material is corrosion, which may be
severe enough to cause breakage, a particularly nasty occurrence in

4 A cross-section through a glassfibre blank showing the large diameter but relatively thin walls of the blank. Glass rods are tough, almost unbreakable, yet very lightweight.

mid-cast. Parallel glass feels much nicer, and the loss in performance is marginal.

Glassfibre blanks have enormous lateral strength but are weak in cross-section. They may be ruined by crushing in a car door, treading on the tip, or even dropping on to rocks. Once cracked, very few blanks are worth mending, because the damage creeps along the blank until it splits wide open. Glassfibre is not immune from rotting either. In the early days of glass technology it was thought that the material would last indefinitely. It does not: after a time it tires and loses strength and speed of cast. Glassfibre also rots if exposed to saltwater, and it must be varnished or painted to keep this out. Once water gets into the weave of the glass matting, the blank seems to unroll itself.

The first glass rods were merely copies of the old designs, and it was not until manufacturers learned to use the material for its own virtues that rods improved. Glass is now worked to its limits, and already thoughts have turned to carbon-fibre. Carbon blanks have proved excellent for flyrods and some freshwater tackle, but their virtues for beachfishing are open to question. All the carbon rods I have used were nice fishing rods, pleasant casting tools and very light for their power. But the difference in performance between carbon and glass is very little; to be honest, I could see no difference at all. In time the new material will supersede glass, but at the moment has little to commend it. In fact the price, at ten times that of glass, is a positive deterrent.

Rod rings

The rings whipped to the blank are guides for the line, but their size and position influence the overall performance of the rod. The weight of the rings added to that of the blank softens the action to some degree; very heavy rings may dampen the rod enough to reduce the cast by 20

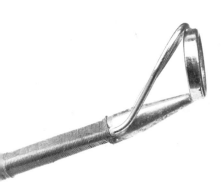

5 *The tip ring—most important of them all. A smooth ring strongly mounted in a steel cradle is essential for shorecasting. The whippings must also be strong, or the ring will fall off under pressure.*

6 *A lightweight hard-chromed steel ring soldered into a neat cradle whipped to the blank with nylon monofilament.*

yds (18 m). Unless taken to those extremes, however, the ring weight is not too important, and it certainly is not worth using light rings purely for weight saving. Good rings, especially those lined with ceramics, tend to be moderately weighty, but the slight loss of cast is more than compensated for by decreased line abrasion.

Ring size is less important than many anglers think. If the line runs nicely from spool to butt ring, through the intermediates and out from the tip without bends, twists or excessive friction, the rings are fine. Very small ones trap weed fragments and are more fragile; very big ones allow the line to flap. Huge rings on rods to be used for casting with fixed-spool reels are a bad choice because the line will twist itself around the rings in midcast with force enough to rip the mountings from the whippings. The idea that big rings make easier, longer casting possible with fixed-spools is nonsense. In fact, tournament casters have proved that small rings increase distance. A good basis for selecting rings for all shorefishing, regardless of the design of reel, is to begin with a 1 in (25 mm) internal diameter at the butt and grade down in $\frac{1}{4}$ in (5 mm) intervals to the tip. The tip diameter will be about $\frac{3}{8}$ in (10 mm) on most normal length rods, but the size of that particular ring can be increased—up to $\frac{5}{8}$ in (15 mm). A slightly bigger ring, with its associated thickness of wire, makes casting and fishing a little smoother.

Too few rings completely destroy the blank's action because the line cannot follow the blank's curve. When the rod bends, the line lies away from it in big chords that jump from ring to ring. The line must stay close, and the number of rings to use, and their position, are determined by this. Experiment is the only guide to correct ringing because so much depends on the action and length combination. A short, flexible rod will need more rings than a stiffer, longer one.

Good rings are of satin-finished hard-chromed steel or stainless steel, and should be hard-soldered or brazed into low-slung mounting cradles of the same materials. The diameter of the ring itself should be moderate, never too slim. Slightly excessive thickness does no harm unless the weight of the set is too high. Ceramic linings are very good indeed; the modern designs are far too efficient to be disregarded, and

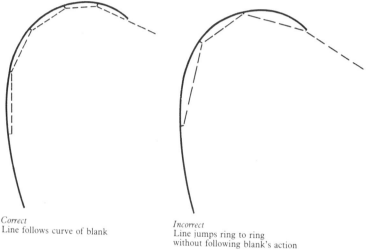

Correct
Line follows curve of blank

Incorrect
Line jumps ring to ring
without following blank's action

Fig 2   Ring positions

are much tougher than the older porcelain liners, which cracked at the slightest excuse. The tip ring is the most important one and must be selected with great care. It carries a great deal of strain and is constantly abraded by line and grit. Small rings are usually too flimsy as well as traps for weeds. The ring itself must be smooth and of large surface area, preferably a ceramic or very hard chrome. Avoid tungsten carbide at all costs: it is exceptionally tough but brittle, snapping at the slightest knock from rock or even shingle. If you should accidentally drop the rod, as you will, the ring will shatter. A broken ring does not matter too much unless it happens to be at the tip, but then its loss brings fishing to an immediate halt.

Rod handles

Not long ago, all fishing rods had cork handles and heavy, chromed winch fittings. For none other than traditional reasons, the reel sat

7 The traditional cork handle and screw winch fitting is still popular because of all the designs, it is the most comfortable to use.

anything from 30 to 40 in (75 to 100 cm) from the butt cap. Lighter and more sporting rods are based on tournament designs, where all superfluous weight is cut away to give a 'bare bones' look. Long cork handles are replaced by plastic sleeving or three simple handgrips, one at the butt and one each side of the reel. The reel is held down by neat sliding catches, or even by hose clips. There is a swing back to the older-style handles of late, but cork has given way to soft composition rubber. Even the winch fitting has undergone change, and is now made of nylon or alloys. The most striking change of all is the shorter handle. The reel is placed 25–30 in (65–75 cm) from the butt, or even lower for those anglers who prefer the South African rod style.

Of all rod handle materials, cork feels nicest. It is warmer and less slippery than the man-made sleevings and handgrips. Its disadvantages are cost, scarcity, and maintenance. Salt penetrates cork and forms into a crust deep inside next to the blank. Glass rots in time, and duralumin corrodes so badly that it finally crumbles and snaps. Rubber and plastics overcome all those problems but are cold and slippery. Their compensations are lightness, neatness and total lack of maintenance.

Reel fittings always seize up, corrode, or just fall off. The fitting that does not hold the reel securely is useless. There have been many attempts at making alternative designs, such as clips and sliders, but nothing rivals the old-fashioned screw and collars. The reel saddle that comes with multipliers is very good too, but if attached directly to the glass blank, the seating should be protected by a strip of rubber, or the glass might be cracked by overtightening.

The materials and basic format of the handle have little effect on the rod's performance and may be chosen according to preference. But the reel position cannot be compromised. It is either right or wrong; and if wrong, may be totally useless. Any rod with a fixed reel fitting should be tested before purchase, because even a few inches too high or low will prevent full-power casts. The handle diameter is worth checking too. Too large a diameter prevents firm grip on the reel's spool for hard casting.

8 A stainless steel sliding reel fitting. An alternative to the screw fitting which is growing in popularity.

9 *The rod should be strong enough to stand up to normal casting and fishing without caving in. This one failed the test.*

Poor quality, badly designed rods are common throughout the world. Few exhibit the correct balance between casting and fishing characteristics. Some mass-produced rods are satisfactory, but the very best are made in limited numbers by specialist companies or by custom builders. Most tackle shops stock rods, produced by major companies, which may be good but are far more likely to be a thoroughly bad investment. Many of the foreign rods—typically Japanese—are excellent in terms of materials and workmanship but they are no good for British shorefishing because the demands of our sport are different from those of the producing nation, for which the equipment was originally designed.

Even so, some of those rods, although seldom ideal, at least permit reasonably good casting and adequate mastery of normal fishing conditions. The rod to look for will be about $11\frac{1}{2}$ ft (3.5 m) in length, moderately fast tapered and capable of bending to its full working curve with 4–6 oz (115–170 g) sinkers cast over average fishing distances. The financial outlay will be modest, and in many respects such a rod is the very best choice for the beginner.

Having fished with it and learned to cast tolerably well, the angler who bought one of those basic rods gains the experience necessary to determine exactly which kind of rod he prefers. Then he can go back to his tackle dealer with a complete list of specifications. Whether he finds a new rod is another matter: many 'specialist' shorefishing rods are far less satisfactory than one would expect. Price and advertised performance do not necessarily reflect quality, or even suitability for shorefishing. Many tackle companies with first class reputations in many branches of the sport fail miserably with saltwater tackle. Some of the extremely expensive rods are, design-wise at least, absolutely useless. It is therefore necessary to search for a supplier who can provide you with the correct rod, or with the materials to make your own.

The ultimate in shorefishing rods is a custom-built rod made up to your specifications. Here again it is important to make sure that you find a good builder, for even the custom-builders are plagued by bungling amateurs who masquerade as experts. You can easily pay the earth for rubbish. As in any other craft, there are some custom-designers and builders who have that indefinable 'something' that puts them into a class of their own. In Britain, the father and son team of Bill and Raymond Roberts are quite unbeatable, and a rod made by them is very desirable indeed. Many of the mass-producers—and more than a few custom designers—take their lead from Bill Roberts' original designs and innovations. Not one of them ever succeeds in matching the quality of the real thing.

2 *Shorecasting reels*

A shorefishing reel has four tasks: it is a line holder, a device that pays out and winds back the line, a braking system to compensate for error, and a firm anchorage so that rod and line have something to lever against.

LINE STORE

Nylon under pressure has a crushing effect measured in tons. After retrieving a heavy sinker through rough ground, or fighting a big fish, line might crush the spool at over 2 tons per square inch (300 kg/cm²). Resilience and rigidity are therefore essential—at least as important as spool capacity. Modern nylon/glass mixtures and lightweight alloys are strong, and if the spool is correctly shaped, there should be little chance of severe damage except by abuse. Some reels are still fitted with bakelite casting spools. These will explode under pressure and must be treated with great respect, even to the extent of slackening the line after a fishing session.

You should find 250 yds (230 m) of line enough for most general shorefishing; it is possible to manage with even less, but then there is no reserve should a big fish decide to run out to sea. The lower the capacity, the smaller the reel, and the easier it is to cast. Sometimes, though, lots of line is vital, even if it does mean shorter casts and more difficult control. Tope and other fast runners can strip 200 yds (180 m) of line in seconds, and unless you have enough on the spool to let them go, your tackle will be smashed. No line will stop a speeding tope dead; you just have to let it have its head.

LINE CONTROL

Because line slips off the rim of a fixed-spool reel, there is less chance of overruns than on a multiplier, where line is paid off from a revolving spool, which, in the case of a really hard cast, might rotate at 30,000 revolutions per minute. Fixed-spool reels are therefore much easier to cast and the logical choice for beginners. The multiplier offers little room for incompetence: if you cast well enough, then it is a lovely tool; if not, expect trouble from the very start.

Many multiplier reels are fitted with casting controls. A common device is a simple brake acting against the spool spindle and controlled by a screw on the bearing cover. More sophisticated are the centrifugal brakes that react to spool revolutions. The brake may be a simple pair of blocks which slide on a bar to press against the brake drum as the reel speeds up, or spring-loaded arms that do much the same thing. One of the simplest, and perhaps best, is a line guide linked to a brake on the outside of the spool. It is rather like a mechanical thumb.

On both multipliers and fixed-spool reels, line pattern has a serious effect on the cast. On multipliers the line should be laid neatly and fairly tight in cotton-reel manner. Automatic level-winds are reasonably good, but they do lower the capacity a little. Also they tend to collect sand and grit in the mechanism, which leads to seizure. The level-wind on fixed-spools is sealed against dirt and thus more reliable, which is a good thing because you can seldom override it.

The gear ratio affects the reel's efficiency. Too high a ratio coupled to a large-diameter spool reduces the mechanical advantage, so that you may not be able to retrieve sinker alone without resorting to line pumping. Small spools and low gearing are more powerful, but the rate of retrieve might then be too slow.

Handle size is another point to watch. A handle that swings in a large arc is efficient but tiring, especially if it throws the reel out of balance. One with a small diameter of rotation cramps and weakens the hand. There is no simple formula for rate of retrieve and handle size; much depends upon the type of fishing. But as a suggestion, handles that swing through a 6–7 in (15–18 cm) circle and pull back about 18 in (45 cm) of line each turn are comfortable and powerful enough for most shore work.

CLUTCH SYSTEM

Some time in the future you will hook a big fish, and for a moment it will gain the upper hand. If the reel clutch does not swing smoothly into action and release line, the tackle will break. That seems a pointless observation: why else have a clutch? Unfortunately, many anglers remember the clutch just after the line snaps. If a survey were taken of British beach fishermen, it would be found that most never used the clutch and that, in some cases, the mechanism had seized up long ago.

Every reel must have a good clutch that allows all settings between free and locked. The lever must be preset so that as soon as pressure in excess of that usually required comes on to the line, the spool releases more. The criteria are smoothness, sensitivity and power; any reel clutch that lacks any of these is not worth fishing with, because it will lose you a big fish. It is also important that the clutch on fixed-spool reels locks the spool for casting; otherwise it rotates in midcast, losing distance and control as the coils of line become buried under one another.

ANCHORAGE

Most of the strains transmitted by fish, water pressure and casting are concentrated on the reel. The strip of metal, the reel seat, that sits in

10 The ideal shorecasting multiplier is smooth-running, robust and with a tough, light spool for easy casting. Simplicity of construction yet high-class workmanship and materials make reels such as this Garcia 602 unbeatable for all-round fishing.

the winch fitting must be strong. Many a fish has been lost and many a cast ruined when the reel seat broke. This part of the reel is particularly vulnerable to corrosion, which creeps into the seams and screw holes. Damage is often hidden and you may not be aware of it until sudden stress rips the reel from the rod.

TYPES OF REEL FOR SHORECASTING

Multiplier reel

ADVANTAGES

1. Gives smooth, very long casting for maximum distance.
2. Sits low on the rod, and thus easy to handle during cast and retrieve.
3. Allows full use of the spool capacity, unless the design is very bad.
4. May be loaded with an exact amount of line to suit the angler's casting style.
5. Gives efficient control of a running fish.
6. May be fitted with a brake to iron out overruns.
7. Is a more pleasant fishing tool, with a nicer feel than the fixed-spool.

DISADVANTAGES

1. Is difficult to control, especially in bad weather and in the dark.
2. Is a nightmare for beginners.
3. Seems, in the case of the more sophisticated reels, to be far more expensive than other types of reel made to the same engineering standards.
4. Requires constant attention to adjustment and maintenance.
5. Has spools that may shatter unless line pressure is carefully controlled.

CHOOSING A MULTIPLIER

Most reels can be ruled out because of their spool design. Nothing matters more than the correct type for both casting and strength. The

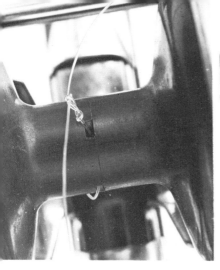

11 *Loading the multiplier (1): secure the line to the spool with a small knot tucked into the slot.*

12 *Loading the multiplier (2): wind on the line in a perfect cotton-reel pattern. Take special care not to create any high spots.*

13 *Loading the multiplier (3): load the spool to the line level determined by experiment (described later) and marked with a small dot of paint. The line is taped down and then the spool is spun to check for uneven lumps and rough running.*

14 *Setting the multiplier: tighten the bearing cap until you can feel a hint of endplay on the bearings and spindle. This is the basic setting; on some reels it may be necessary to tighten the bearing so that the reel is more controllable.*

spool should be reasonably small, light and able to withstand pressure. Reinforced plastics and light alloys are best; heavy brass is intolerable for casting because of the flywheel effect, which makes control impossible. Bakelite spools are worst of all for exploding under stress, which is a pity because many otherwise perfect reels are fitted with them. Line may be accommodated on either a wide, shallow spool, or a deep, narrow one. The choice is personal, provided that you can stretch your thumb far enough to hold down the latter. Spools of similar capacity but different design have a similar casting performance, although a deep spool may be fractionally better with the heavier leads for casting very long distances.

The spool spindle must be strong, polished and absolutely straight. Any imbalance or roughness reduces cast distances and boosts wear. The bearings may be either plain bushes or ballraces. On the beach there is little difference in their relative performances, but ballraces make the reel much smoother and silky. Never buy reels without oil ports in the bearing caps, because regular lubrication is essential.

Many anglers struggle with free-running multipliers and eventually resort to a control device. Their reluctance to use one in the first place is because they have read or heard that the best casters use a totally free spool. All the world's best casters use reel controls. Many use a centrifugal system, either by itself or further smoothed by specially selected oils. Nobody, but nobody, can cast a reel that is not governed down in some way.

Despite controls, overruns are inevitable. It helps to have a reel that comes apart so that spools can be interchanged as required. Several quick-take-apart systems are in use, but they all have disadvantages. Bayonet-fitting sideplates are very good when new, but when the reel begins to corrode and the constant fishing pressure warps the reel cage, the system jams. There is nothing simpler and more reliable than the sideplate fastening that uses big screws which may be loosened with the edge of a coin.

Fixed-spool reel

ADVANTAGES

1. Is very easy to cast, with a shoreline performance close to the multiplier's.
2. Can be used with confidence at night and in bad weather.
3. Has automatic line spread to ensure constant pattern.
4. Is better value for money than the multiplier.
5. Is less demanding in adjustment and maintenance.
6. Has less tendency to burst spools.
7. Casts very light sinkers that the multiplier cannot handle.
8. Is the choice for normal spinning and floatfishing.

DISADVANTAGES

1. Suffers from poor retrieve, further hampered by imbalance.

2. Has gearing far too high for normal leger work.
3. Prevents use of much of the line capacity, because of the spool shape.
4. Twists line.
5. Has a spool which has to be locked for casting.
6. May cut your fingers in hard casting unless they are protected in some way, or the rod is fitted with a release device.

CHOOSING A FIXED-SPOOL REEL

The best reel is the one that holds the right amount of line and is as small and compact as possible. Shorefishing fixed-spool reels are the very worst designed tackle on the market. It is no stretch of the imagination to suppose that most were never designed at all: they are simply scaled-up freshwater reels. They are far too big and heavy. The gearing is too high—so high that most cannot retrieve a 6 oz (170 g) sinker without pumping. Spool shape is wrong and lip friction so great that casting range is reduced unless the reel is absolutely crammed with line.

But having said all that, let me continue by suggesting that most anglers would save time, frustration and cash by using fixed-spool reels. They are easy to use, almost overrun-free, and put an end to the misery caused by multiplier reels in unskilled hands. The principle of the reel is excellent; the casting performance is for all practical purposes equal to that of the multiplier—except into headwinds, where it is actually better. So many huge fishes have been tamed on fixed-spools that their fighting ability need never be questioned.

No, the trouble is the way in which the reels are made. It is not possible simply to magnify a freshwater reel, then expect it to perform well in the sea where the demands are totally different. The gearing and retrieve rate should suit heavy terminal tackle. Spools should be shaped so as to throw off line without excessive friction. Overall, the reel could be lightened and shortened to improve balance. One enlightened company has begun work on a special seafishing reel that overcomes many of the current objections. The prototype I handled was an absolute dream; if it comes on to the market I would bet that it cuts the ground from under the feet of other fixed-spools and multipliers also. But at the moment it is a case of picking the reel that is least bad. True, it will be tiring and uncomfortable, but you at least have the satisfaction of trouble-free fishing.

Sidecast reel

There is a reel that casts like a fixed-spool, but afterwards the spool turns through a right angle so that the line is wound back centre-pin reel fashion. There is only one reel of this type on the British market: and it is called the Alvey, and is Australian in origin. It is a superb reel, but unfortunately one that does not enjoy the success it merits. Perhaps its rather dated appearance and complete lack of charisma account for its apparently limited sales. That is a shame: the Alvey casts supremely well and is a very good fishing tool also.

LOADING REELS WITH LINE

No reel works well unless it is correctly loaded. The line should be reasonably tight, but not so stretched that the spool is at risk. The knot attaching the line to the spool core must be strong but neat. Any backing materials should be carefully selected and applied. Never attempt to wind on the line unless the reel is firmly mounted on a rod.

Fixed-spool reels

Most of these reels need extra backing because of their bad spool shape. It is essential that the line level is maintained within ⅛ in (3 mm) of the spool lip (fig 3) in order to minimise friction. Insufficient line creates friction so severe that the casting range might be cut by half. Overfilling is permissible for ultra-long casting, but an overloaded spool is difficult to control as line tries to spring off.

Every fixed-spool reel twists line. Swivels are useless for preventing a build-up of coils. Eventually the whole line becomes so kinked that as soon as it flies off the spool it tangles into knots. The easy way to comb it out is to take the reel into a field of grass, let out all the line, then drag it through the grass for a few hundred yards. All the twists disappear, and when rewound the line is as good as new.

Multiplier reels

Line levels on the multiplier are as critical as on the other types of reels. In some respects they are even more important, because every caster must find a capacity which suits his cast. The only way to find the

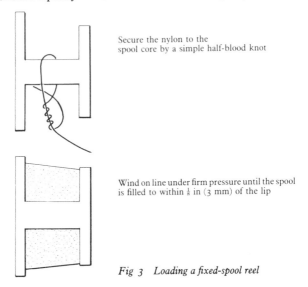

Secure the nylon to the spool core by a simple half-blood knot

Wind on line under firm pressure until the spool is filled to within ⅛ in (3 mm) of the lip

Fig 3   Loading a fixed-spool reel

correct level is by experiments that will be described later in the book. Reels for shorefishing rarely need backing; if they do, the spool, and consequently the whole reel, is too big. Tie the end of the nylon to the spool core as neatly as possible, using the slot if one is provided (fig 4). Wind on the line cotton-reel fashion, laying each coil snugly against its neighbour. Build up slowly and carefully: there must be no humps and hollows in the spool. The final 150 yds may be wound on less meticulously, but there must be every attempt to fill the spool as well as practically possible. Any high spot will form a heavy area which throws the spool out of balance. Even a few misplaced coils affect a whirling spool; if the problem is severe, the whole reel will judder and overrun. After the reel is full, cut off the end of the line and tape it against the spool. Spin the reel and watch for any uneven patches. Unless the spool runs true, strip off all the line and start again.

MAINTENANCE

Most reels are well engineered, with accurately cut gears and closely mating surfaces. The materials are either plastics (and reinforced composites) or corrosion-proofed metals. The seashore is no respecter of fine craftsmanship: sand and salt work their way into the reel, and in the long term even proofed materials succumb. Nobody who fishes regularly should expect his tackle to retain its pristine appearance, but it is still necessary to cleanse and lubricate it at intervals to ensure smooth working. It is too easy to return from fishing and leave the reel soaking wet with seawater. It will keep working for many months, but hidden damage may have occurred: the screws and reel seat may have developed a crust of salty deposit, or a few particles of sand may be

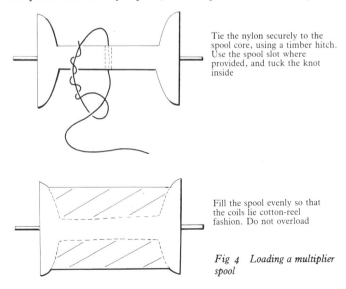

Tie the nylon securely to the spool core, using a timber hitch. Use the spool slot where provided, and tuck the knot inside

Fill the spool evenly so that the coils lie cotton-reel fashion. Do not overload

Fig 4   Loading a multiplier spool

15 A beachcasting fixed-spool reel. The most important factor is line level. The line must be about ⅛ in (3 mm) from the lip, or casting becomes a problem because of excessive friction. The reel here is used in conjunction with a release device that sits on the rod and holds the line for casting. Lifting the thumb releases the line and therefore avoids sore fingers.

grinding away at the gears. One day the reel comes under strain: a really big fish takes hold of the bait, perhaps. Then the reel jams solid. The brake will not work. The line tightens . . . and snap.

Regular care takes a few moments. Take off the spool and wipe it clean; wash the reel with hot, soapy water, then rinse it under the hot tap. Dry it overnight in the airing cupboard. Dab a spot of oil in multiplier bearings and on the spool spindle. Reassemble the reel, spray it with aerosol lubricant, and rub it over with a cloth. Best of all is a good squirt of WD40 fluid which drives out water and gives a protective film. If the reel is regularly checked, repairs on the shore should be rarely necessary. But should you drop the reel into sand, there is only one remedy: wash the reel in the sea, then use your spare one to finish the day.

A SIX-MONTHLY SCHEDULE

1. Strip off all the line and discard it.
2. Wash off all surface dirt with hot, soapy water.
3. Strip the reel into its major components. Do not take things apart unless you are sure how they go back.
4. Clean out all the old dirt and stale grease. Use an old toothbrush to clear out awkward crevices.
5. Spray everything with very hot water, then allow to dry.
6. Examine the reel for broken or worn parts.
7. Replace or repair these as necessary.
8. Repack parts with grease where required. Lubricate spool bearings with 90 grade gear oil.
9. Reassemble, then tighten all screws and nuts.

16 *A multiplier stripped for maintenance. It is normally sufficient to strip down only this far; too much dismantling may lead to trouble unless you are absolutely sure how all the parts fit together.*

17 *The bale arm roller on a fixed-spool reel is subject to enormous pressure and abrasion. Unless it rolls, wear will be rapid and could create a groove that actually cuts through the nylon.*

18 *The internal mechanism of a fixed-spool. With all its precision engineering and liberal coating of grease, it is easy to see why a few specks of grit can play havoc.*

10. Adjust the controls. Make sure that the clutch is fairly slack on reels to be stored; otherwise, set at the correct pressure for the line's breaking strain.

11. Refill the spool with line.

12. If something goes wrong and you cannot get the reassembled mechanism to work, take the reel to a repairer. It is quicker and cheaper in the long run. Many anglers wreck a reel, then take it back to the shop complaining that 'It just fell apart in my hands'—sneaky, and not to be recommended.

3 Sinkers and lines

FUNCTION OF SINKERS

The heavy sinker on the end of his line enables the shorefisherman to cast and sink his baits. Fierce tides and offshore currents, wind and air resistance of tackle influence the choice. As far as many anglers are concerned any old chunk of lead will do. In fact, sinkers require careful consideration. Weight and shape must be matched to sea and weather conditions, bait size, expected distance and to the physique and casting style of the angler himself. The rest of the tackle must be balanced to the sinker, not vice versa.

DESIGN OF SINKERS

Design takes into account the two main functions. The sinker is a heavy mass that sinks terminal tackle and baits into the sea and holds them anchored to the seabed or suspended at controlled depth beneath a float. Driven to high speed by the rod, a flying sinker is transformed into an enormous propulsive force that rockets out to sea during the cast.

It is generally supposed that a fast-moving sinker needs the same attention to aerodynamics and ballistics as do bullets and aircraft. In practice the same rules do not apply: a sinker moves relatively slowly, hampered by the drag of reel, line and baits. Experiments on the casting field with no baits or traces to aggravate drag show that sinker streamlining improves distances by less than 5 per cent. This gain must be compared to the losses that baits inflict upon normal fishing casts. One worm and a single hook paternoster cut potential distances by 15–25 per cent.

Weight alone is sufficient to prevent tackle drift in calm water, but in fast tides and strong lateral currents, line pressure sweeps the tackle ashore unless the sinker is modified so that it digs in like an anchor. Ordinary casting sinkers may be modified by moulding into the nose a set of long, curved gripwires to give a grapnel effect. An alternative to this is to use a sinker shaped like an inverted pyramid, which ploughshares its way into soft sand and mud.

Sinker shape also affects the smooth working of float tackle. Drilled bullets and bombs slide on the line with minimum risk of tangling with the trace. The combination of large bait, bulky float and heavy sinker

19 The most commonly used sinkers for shorefishing. From left to right, the casting sinker, the pyramid sinker for sand and mud, and the gripwire sinker used to hold the tackle against water pressure.

20 A casting sinker fitted with collapsible wires. During casting and fishing the wires are held in position by the rubber band. When the tackle is retrieved, the extra line pressure triggers the band and the wires flip over to trail the sinker. Retrieve is then much easier and less strain on the tackle.

tends to whirl around in midair. A neat sinker is less likely to ensnare the line than one attached by a loop of wire at one end.

WEIGHT OF SINKERS

Unless absolute casting distance is the only factor that determines success—as it often does—sinker weight is best kept to the minimum compatible with wind, sea and bait size. From a sportsman's point of view, light tackle offers more fun than very heavy equipment which merely drags the fish ashore. In calm waters and at short range, light tackle may be used to advantage; 1 oz (30 g) of lead may be all that is required to cast and sink the baits. In rough seas and into the teeth of a gale, more weight has to be clipped on to the line so that baits can be anchored. The rest of the tackle has to be stepped up to compensate.

As a rule of thumb, try using 1 oz (a sparing 30 g) of sinker weight for every Beaufort point of windspeed. Fishing into a Force 6 wind is easier with 6 oz (170 g) than it would be with less. Sea conditions are sometimes independent of the wind, but the sinker has to match the sea, not the weather, in that case. Small sinkers swirl around in heavy swells and may never reach the bottom in deep water. Floatfishing is bound by the same rules: sometimes 6 or even 8 oz (170 or 225 g) are necessary to drag the baits deep enough.

Firm anchorage does more than hold the baits steady. Experienced cod anglers know that for some reason cod prefer baits clamped to the seabed. Big, heavy grip-sinkers are used as routine by many cod fishermen regardless of sea and weather conditions. They have proved to their own satisfaction that heavy tackle hooks more fish. In commercial fishing, longliners are most careful to anchor their lines as close to the bottom as possible. In addition to an anchor at each end, the line is pegged at regular intervals with secondary weights. Any baited hook left flapping in the tide is less likely to produce a cod.

Nine times out of ten the sinker hooks the fish for you. Anglers employ all manner of elaborate striking methods. Any of them is a waste of time and energy at a range of more than 50 yds (45 m). The fish usually hooks itself by snatching at the bait and moving off with it until the tethered trace brings it up short. If the initial shock alone does not drive home the hook, the sudden clout from the trace certainly will. If you get the sinker anchored hard against the bottom, in most cases your fish will be hooked neatly in the jaw or throat. Sinkers that skid and roll along the seabed lead to missed bites, or fish with the hook down in their guts. Unless the situation demands moving baits, firm anchorage increases catches.

TYPES OF SINKER FOR SHOREFISHING

Casting sinkers

Most British anglers use bomb or pear-shaped sinkers attached to the line by a wire loop moulded in at one end (fig 5). The range of weights is from 1 to 16 oz (30 to 455 g), the most useful being 2–8 oz (55–225 g). Regular fishermen, especially those who fish rough ground, are well advised to make their own sinkers. Moulds, scrap lead and wires are available from tackle shops and metal dealers; and the savings are tremendous. Moulding sinkers is easy and safe enough provided that you remember one thing: molten lead and cold, damp moulds just don't mix. You can end up showered with red-hot lead particles.

Many anglers mould in fixed gripwires as routine. They may be left

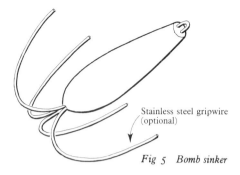

Stainless steel gripwire
(optional)

Fig 5 Bomb sinker

straight if not required for anchorage. Gripwires claw into the ground and sometimes hold so well that the tackle is strained. To overcome that, a collapsible wire device has been designed (fig 6). The grips are held in place by a rubber band for casting and fishing, but on the retrieve, the extra pressure springs the band and the wires, which are hinged, flip backwards to trail the sinker.

Pyramid sinkers

This type of sinker is a pyramid of lead with a long loop sprouting from the centre of its square base (fig 7). It casts well, and once in the water acts like a ploughshare. It will hold against moderate currents, and is at its best over soft sand and mud. Hard seabeds of clay, shale and compacted sand do not afford sufficient grip. Pyramids are particularly useful for surf-fishing where there are no fierce currents. The sinker digs in just enough to jerk the trace when a fish bites. The sinkers are usually less than 4 oz (115 g) in weight. Beyond that, the gripwired bomb is far better.

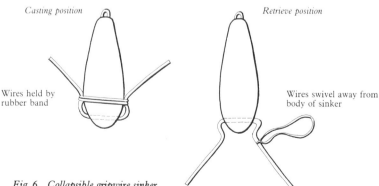

Casting position

Wires held by
rubber band

Retrieve position

Wires swivel away from
body of sinker

36 *Fig 6 Collapsible gripwire sinker*

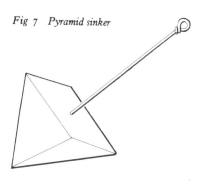

Fig 7   Pyramid sinker

Drilled bullets and bombs

Small round bullets and bombs with a hole drilled right through the centre are useful for floatfishing, spinning and very light legering. The weights range from $\frac{1}{4}$ to 4 oz (7 to 115 g).

Lead sheeting and lead wire

Small sheets and slivers of lead make useful sinkers that you can fold on to the line without having to take apart the tackle. They are useful when you want just a little more weight on float or spinning tackles to sink the baits deeper.

LINES

The line is the only link between the fisherman on the beach and his baits, which might be up to 150 yds (140 m) away. You would think that because of the great distance, the effects of the tide and the possibility of hooking a big fish, the line ought to be very strong. Shorefishing tackle is, however, easier to use and far more efficient when line diameter and breaking strain are cut to a safe minimum.

There is a simple experiment to show just how little strain the rod exerts on the line. Take your rod and reel into a field and run out 150

21 The pyramid sinker holds the tackle by digging its way into the sand in ploughshare fashion.

yds (or 150 m) of line. Tie the end to a fence post, then go back to the rod and pull as hard as you can. You will find it impossible to break the line; in fact, you will give up because the rod seems likely to snap first. Go back to the far end of the line and insert a short piece of 5 lb (2.3 kg) line between the reel line and the post. Rod pressure fails to break it. The knots that join the light line to the post and reel line have reduced the overall breaking strain to less than 4 lb (1.8 kg), but still you cannot win. Reduce the distance by 30 yds (or 30 m) and try again. Keep moving up in 10 yd (or 10 m) intervals until the line breaks. The distance from you to the post is probably less than 50 yds (45 m). By substituting a spring balance for the weaker line, you would find that a normal beachcasting rod registers 2–3 lb (0.9–1.4 kg) at 100 yds (90 m) plus, 5–7 lb (2.3–3.2 kg) at 50 yds (45 m) and little more than 10 lb (4.5 kg) at 20 yds (18 m). Another experiment: try to lift a 15 lb (6.8 kg) deadweight on the rod.

It is physically impossible with ordinary shorefishing tackle to use the full performance of more than 10 lb (4.5 kg) breaking strain. However, it would be hazardous to use a line this thin for normal shorecasting because other factors influence selection. Every beach, rock platform, estuary and harbour has obstructions which cut and abrade lines. Even sand and mud grind them. Thin nylon, having a relatively large surface area for its breaking strain, rapidly loses strength. On stepping up the diameter, the surface area becomes relatively less for a considerable increase in breaking strain, and is therefore more resistant to abrasion. On the other hand, there is no point using too thick a line because the rod cannot exploit its strength.

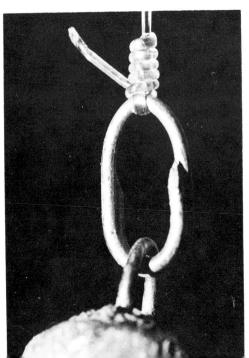

22 The split ring is essential to buffer the sinker-line joint against abrasion by sand and shingle. Attaching the line directly to the sinker is dangerous because the knot is ground away until it snaps in midcast.

In practice, long-range shorecasting is best with nylon monofilament lines between 15 and 20 lb (6.8 and 9.1 kg) breaking strain. Braided Dacron, Terylene and nylons can be useful from the beach, but only at short range where their lack of stretch may be of advantage, as in conger fishing. Another reason for almost doubling the theoretical 10 lb (4.5 kg) lower limit is the strange things that happen when big fish run long distances. For some obscure reason, probably to do with water drag, even strong lines will snap as the fish tears through the tide.

Of course, it is sometimes impractical to use the standard weight lines. Spinning and light float tackle would be stifled by even 18 lb (8.2 kg) nylon, so 10 lb (4.5 kg) would be a better choice, though it would need careful and regular checking for abrasion. Sometimes you need very powerful tackle. Imagine how it is to hook a big conger eel right under your feet beneath a pier. The fish feels the hook and makes straight for the piles. If he gets there, his tail will whip around the nearest obstruction, and then your task is to raise him from the ocean floor. You have to pull harder than he can; so you select a short rod and very strong line—say, 50 lb (22.7 kg) Dacron, which has the advantage of no stretch.

A 15–20 lb (6.8–9.1 kg) line combines adequate strength with minimal diameter. The diameter, and hence the cross-sectional area, affects both sinker weight and tackle size. Water pressure on 100 yds (90 m) of line lying across a spring ebb is considerable, and the only way to prevent drifting is firm anchorage. The thicker the line, the greater the pressure; so you need a big sinker, which in turn has to be cast on a powerful rod. A vicious circle is soon established which makes fishing a nightmare. But by standardising on, say, 18 lb (8.2 kg) line with a diameter of 0.017 in (0.45 mm), you can throw normal 4–6 oz (115–170 g) sinkers vast distances and anchor against the strongest tide by using light rods and small reels. Fishing and casting are difficult enough without the extra burden of crane-like tackle.

CASTING LEADERS

Nylon line in good condition and properly tied copes with normal fishing strains. The standard casting lines are most unlikely to break except through abuse. Nevertheless, they cannot withstand the initial shock of powerful casting. A good caster using powerful tackle and a 6 oz (170 g) sinker can snap 30 lb (13.6 kg) line as if it were cotton.

It is unnecessary to use strong line throughout, because the initial shock of the cast affects the first few feet only. After the reel is released, line pressure falls almost to zero while the sinker is in flight. Ideally, a line for shorefishing would combine small diameter with high breaking strain. (Although we use lower-breaking-strain line it is chiefly for its low diameter, not simply for low strength. There is no objection to an extremely powerful line as long as it is thin enough for casting.) The ideal line does not yet exist, and the only way to achieve high initial breaking strain is by attaching a short length of strong line to the reel line itself. The piece is known as a casting or shock leader, and is

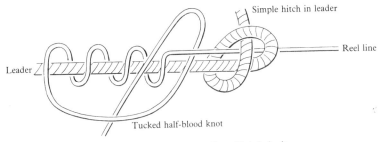

Simple hitch in leader

Reel line

Leader

Tucked half-blood knot

1 Form hitch in leader
2 Pass reel line through loop
3 Pull hitch tight with pliers
4 Tie blood knot
5 Tighten the line and trim the loose ends leaving ⅛ in (3 mm) of free nylon on each

Fig 8   Leader attachment

normally about 10 yds (9 m) long. The knot is specially chosen so as not to catch in the rings. Leader strength depends on the caster's power and his sinker. The following is a guide to leader weights for shorecasting:

SINKER WEIGHT		LEADER BREAKING STRAIN	
oz	g	lb	kg
2	55	15	6.8
3	85	25	11.3
4	115	35	15.8
5	140	40	18.1
6	170	45	20.4
8	225	50	22.7

4 *Terminal tackle*

Rods and reels are not the most important equipment. It is possible to dispense with them and still catch fish. Of course, they do make fishing easier and more fun; and a good rod and reel are essential for long-range casting. Casting and retrieving line is effortless with the right tackle, but the tackle that catches fish is the terminal rig. It is the third most important factor in angling, following closely behind natural history and good baits.

THE FUNCTIONS OF TERMINAL TACKLE

1. To present the bait as a trap.
2. To allow presentation at any depth.
3. To assist long-distance casting.

Presentation

It is nonsense to suggest that baits must appear natural. Worms seldom drift in midwater or occur as massed bunches; mackerel fillets are rare in nature; Californian squid are alien to the diet of a North Sea cod. Fish pick up baits because they are stimulated to do so, or merely curious. Life in the sea is hard; there is a constant fight for survival which means that no opportunity may be missed. Fish investigate anything that might turn out to be food, and anglers' baits are just one item in a very long list of possibilities.

Fish in aquaria may be observed to pick up stones, bits of weed and floating debris, which are sucked, then either eaten or ejected. Mullet in harbours are seen to do the same thing, and it is reasonable to assume that most other species share the habit. That being so, a fish will examine a baited hook for no better reason than that it just happens to be lying there. The scavenging theory is borne out by the stomach contents of many fishes. It is not uncommon to find bits of rubbish, coal, orange peel and even discarded British Rail teacups inside a cod.

Baits should be absolutely fresh and mounted to form efficient traps. Correct mounting and proper hook size catch more fish because the hookpoint is not buried in superfluous tissues. A fish can pick up, swallow immediately and hook itself without first having to reduce the bait to a manageable size.

Depth

Different species of fishes patrol at different, fixed depths, which they are normally reluctant to change because it takes them away from their natural habitat. Deepwater wrasse lurking among the weeds and rocks of seabed valleys will not rise even 6 ft (1.8 m) for baits floated overhead. Pollack and other midwater predators prefer a fixed patrol depth which may alter from day to day, but not hourly. The terminal rig must be selected to present the bait at precisely controlled depth: on the seabed, midwater or just under the surface. The raw winds and racing tides of a winter cod beach demand firm bait anchorage, or the line and tackle will be swept ashore within seconds. Wrasse and deepwater bass ambush slowly drifting bait suspended beneath a float. Garfish in a tiderace pick off their prey as it hurtles along in the current, but ignore stationary baits. Leger, float and spinning rigs take all these preferences into account. The nature of the seabed influences choice: rocky ground is a graveyard for legers. Usually it is possible to compromise by using a rig that suits both the fish and the nature of the ground. But if that is impractical the rig must favour presentation, and tackle losses accepted with good grace.

Long-distance casting

Casting introduces more problems. Bait presentation and position must be preserved, but air resistance has to be cut or the tackle falls short. Again, a compromise is necessary: if the bait is 50 yds (45 m) short of the mark it is absolutely useless. Although not a perfect solution, it is better to cast a less attractive bait all the way out. A poor bait in the right place at least stands some chance of being taken. Fortunately, many of the long-range fishing beaches are better covered by a simple paternoster, which allows good casting anyway. Cod and whiting beaches are an excellent example; the fish are usually so voracious that second-rate presentation makes little difference.

If it is necessary to throw long distances with running leger tackle, the baits may be streamlined and tied down to the trace by strips of the water-soluble plastic, polyvinyl alcohol (PVA). Such rigs cut air resistance considerably and allow casts of up to 25 per cent longer than otherwise possible. Air drag and distance losses are further reduced by increasing sinker weight.

TYPES OF TERMINAL TACKLE RIG

Paternoster

The simplest and most common rig for all-round seafishing, the paternoster is cheap and easy to produce, casts extremely well and places baits right down on the seabed. The tackle may be anchored or allowed to drift in the tide. Up to three hooks are used, all baited differently if you are unsure of the right choice, or loaded identically if the fishes are so co-operative that they bite three at a time. Single-hook

23 *A bass caught from the surf on paternoster tackle. The fish was hooked well over 100 yd (90 m) offshore, and any other tackle rig might have made such long casting almost impossible.*

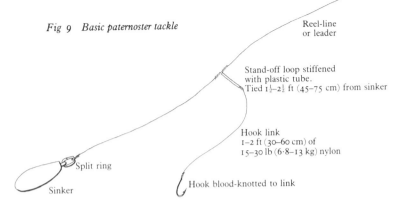

Fig 9   Basic paternoster tackle

Reel-line or leader

Stand-off loop stiffened with plastic tube.
Tied 1½–2½ ft (45–75 cm) from sinker

Hook link
1–2 ft (30–60 cm) of
15–30 lb (6·8–13 kg) nylon

Split ring

Sinker

Hook blood-knotted to link

rigs cast farther and allow really big baits to be cast well over 130 yds (120 m). Modified with PVA, a single-hook paternoster enables very good casters to place their baits up to 160 yd (145 m) in perfect weather.

Running Leger

The principle behind this rig is to allow fish to make off with the bait without feeling any resistance from trace or line. This may happen in calm water, although even then its importance is questionable. In fast tides, where the reel line is under pressure, the rig cannot work as intended and you might just as well use a simple paternoster with a long link between hook and line. Very long flowing traces are sometimes good for fishing tiny baits at short range, but the air resistance and awkwardness of casting makes them very inefficient at more than 100 yds (90 m) range, even if PVA packaging is used. In practice there is usually so little to choose between them and the paternoster that the latter rig could be used instead. Running traces are far more expensive to produce and no more effective except in a very few instances. Special

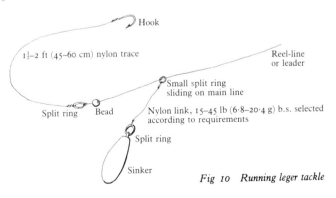

Hook

1½–2 ft (45–60 cm) nylon trace

Reel-line or leader

Small split ring sliding on main line

Split ring   Bead

Nylon link, 15–45 lb (6·8–20·4 g) b.s. selected according to requirements

Split ring

Sinker

Fig 10   Running leger tackle

sliders called Kilmore and Clements booms are available as substitutes for the cheaper split ring. Their expense would be justified if they worked well. But they do not, and as all shorefishermen lose tackle, it is perhaps wiser to forget about them. A useful modification for the rig is a piece of cork attached just above the hook. It holds the baits above the seabed out of the reach of crabs and shrimps.

Tope and conger eel tackle

Tope and conger are two British species that merit special terminal tackles. Tope are members of the shark family, sharing with their cousins the powerful jaws and sharp teeth of the sea's greatest predatory species. Tope and eels wrap themselves in the trace and very soon snap ordinary reel lines. A strong casting leader made up of 5 yds (4.5 m) of 50 lb (22.7 kg) line backed by the same length of 30 lb (13.6 kg) is

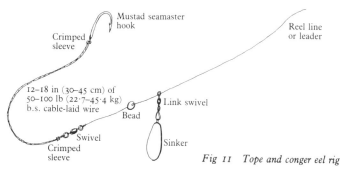

Fig 11   Tope and conger eel rig

additional to a short trace of cable-laid wire. Basically, the arrangement is similar to the running leger with swivels substituting for split rings. Swivels are expensive, seldom rotate under pressure, and are completely unnecessary for routine fishing, but tope and conger rigs have to withstand so much pressure and abrasion that anything which might increase durability is worth having—even swivels. Very good quality ball-bearing swivels iron out line twist and avoid kinks in the trace wire. Kinked wire loses at least 70 per cent of its breaking strain. Weakness cannot be tolerated with conger eels that fight a war of attrition in gullies and rock piles, which themselves abrade the tackle. Conger eels and tope also merit a special hook, because lesser designs may well snap or straighten under severe strain. The best hook on the British market is Mustad's Seamaster. The hooks are attached to trace wire by crimping metal sleeves on to the wire. Knots alone are never to be used.

Lightweight floatfishing tackle

Light float tackle with a 1 oz (30 g) sinker drifts baits down to the wrasse or up nearer the surface for pollack, mackerel and midwater species of all kinds. Tackle losses over rough ground are minimised; in

Fig 12   Lightweight floatfishing tackle

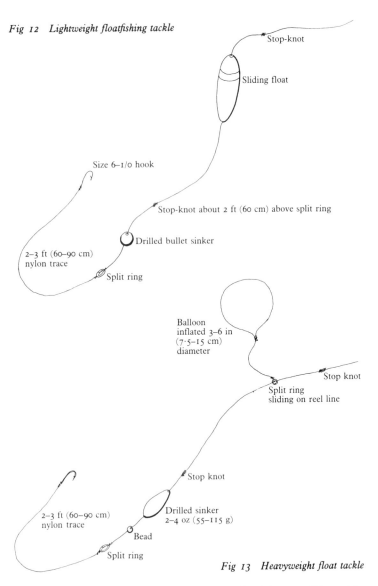

Stop-knot

Sliding float

Size 6–1/0 hook

Stop-knot about 2 ft (60 cm) above split ring

Drilled bullet sinker

2–3 ft (60–90 cm) nylon trace

Split ring

Balloon inflated 3–6 in (7·5–15 cm) diameter

Stop knot

Split ring sliding on reel line

Stop knot

Drilled sinker 2–4 oz (55–115 g)

2–3 ft (60–90 cm) nylon trace

Bead

Split ring

Fig 13   Heavyweight float tackle

fact, the tackle opens up miles of otherwise unfishable coast. The tackle assembly is simple but you can make a few modifications. There is no need to use proper floats; cubes of polystyrene foam, old film containers and discarded table-tennis balls can be pressed into service and they are every bit as good as floats bought from the shops. The most important part of the rig is the lower stop knot which prevents the float from

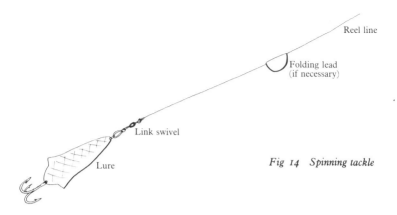

Reel line

Folding lead
(if necessary)

Link swivel

Lure

Fig 14   Spinning tackle

sliding too close to the sinker and tangling. When that happens in midcast, the baits are fished just under the surface regardless of the set depth. A 1 in (2.5 cm) strip of elastic band clove-hitched to the line will arrest all but the heaviest float tackle.

Heavyweight float tackle

Heavy float tackle is scaled up from the normal arrangement for use where long casting is essential, or for big fish and correspondingly large baits. Water and weather conditions sometimes prevent lighter tackle from reaching full depth; 2 or even 4 oz (55 or 115 g) of lead may be necessary to overcome the tide, swells and wind. Another use of heavy float tackle is in suspended-line fishing, which will be described in detail later.

Spinning tackle and feathers

Artificial lure rigs are the simplest of all. It is necessary only to attach the spinner or lure to the reel line, perhaps using a swivel or split ring for convenience. If additional sinker weight is demanded, as in rough seas and for long casting, a small piece of lead is threaded or clipped on about 1 yd (0.9 m) up the trace. Extra weight should be avoided if possible, because anything fixed to the line muffles the action of the lure. Special trace material is required over rough ground and for sharp-toothed species like ling. A short leader of stronger nylon is blood-knotted to the reel line, or a short piece of lightweight wire is crimped on between line and lure. Commercial lures are fitted with treble hooks, but some anglers prefer to take them off and attach ordinary single hooks. Single hooks are better if the lure is baited, and besides, they are less likely to catch in weeds.

Strings of feathers are cast out on paternoster tackle and worked through the water in sink-and-draw style. Feathering from the shore is a rough and ready way to catch fish with little pretence of sport. It is a **47** bait collection technique that lets you hook a dozen mackerel in a couple of casts.

Freeline tackle

If you are fishing at very close range in still water, why bother about terminal rigs? Just tie on a hook and cast the bait under its own weight. Freelined baits offer no resistance to a feeding fish, cost next to nothing, and are in many ways the best rig of all. They are capable of being used far more often than you would suppose. The natural progression from the rig is flyfishing tackle. Flyfishing techniques and equipment can be modified to suit British seafishing, and although we lack the gamefish that make the technique so popular overseas, there is room for experiment. Mackerel and garfish on flyrods are great fun.

MATERIALS FOR TERMINAL TACKLE ASSEMBLY

Lines

Ordinary nylon line for hook links, traces and leaders should be chosen to match the fishing. Often the breaking strain is equal to that of the line, or slightly less. If its purpose is to buffer against abrasion, it

24 Even new hooks need sharpening. This hook is new from the packet but too blunt to drive into a fish's tough mouth. A few strokes on the stone will make it needle-sharp, but it will need careful checking later on because stones and rock soon dull it again.

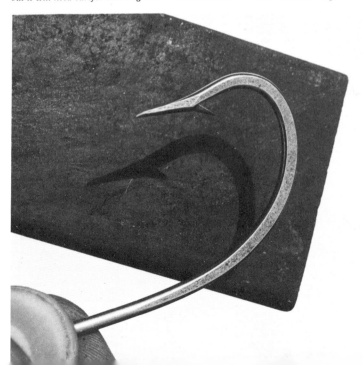

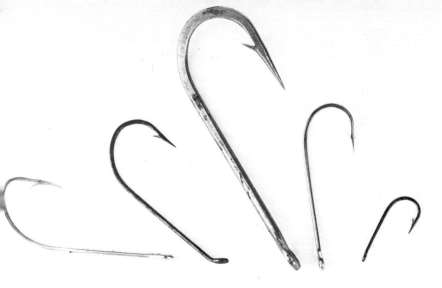

25 A selection of shorefishing hooks from size 2 up to 6/o. Reasonably fine wire hooks are best for most fishing but tough species need really strong hooks of rather coarse stainless wire. The exact hook design is almost irrelevant: there are thousands of designs on the market and one's choice is personal, assuming of course that size, shank length and bend are suitable for the bait in use.

should be thicker. Nylon lines may be joined directly or via a split ring or swivel. Never tie a long-distance casting sinker directly to the leader, because sand and grit wear down the knot, which then snaps in midcast. The knots for joining nylon to hooks, split rings, swivels and other nylon are blood knots and their derivatives.

Hooks

The versatile angler carries a range of hooks between sizes 8 and 6/o. Normally, hook size is determined by the baits and the species of fish to be caught. Big hooks are not necessarily better at holding big fish. Small, sharp hooks of high quality are more than a match for any fish that swims in British waters. Always buy the best available. Cheap ones are undertempered or too brittle, and will either snap or straighten out. Neither size nor design really matters if the hook suits the bait and is really sharp. Long and short shanks have their uses: long for worm baits and fillets, shorter for smaller baits like shellfish, and for the big predators which can use a hook shank as a lever to spring the point. There are several thousand designs of hook shape; all have their devotees, but none is proved to be superior to the rest. It is a question of personal preference in most cases. I personally use the Mustad

Viking range; on the other hand I would not be happy fishing with the long-shanked, very fine wire hooks some anglers like for worms.

Swivels and split rings

If you wish to waste money on expensive tackle that serves no purpose, buy swivels. Shore-fishermen seldom require them to smooth out twists: normal fishing does not kink lines and the coils created by a fixed-spool reel are better removed by a special process of combing out the line. The trouble with swivels is most of them do not rotate, and are therefore no more than a link. If you need a link, split rings are the answer: they are a tenth the cost, stronger, less likely to break from poor manufacture or inferior materials, and do not corrode internally as swivels do. Very high quality big-game swivels do work properly, but these need be used for tope and congers only.

Trace wire

Nylon-covered, cable-laid stainless wire is a tough trace material for species with very sharp teeth. Tope, conger eels, some rays and the bigger ling will cut through ordinary nylon traces and do require the extra protection of wire. Seafishing wire is available in breaking strains from 7 lb (3.2 kg) to over 100 lb (45.4 kg). Three sizes cover most work: 20 lb (9.1 kg) for inshore ling and small congers, 50 lb (22.6 kg) for general heavy fishing, and 100 lb (45.4 kg) for very big tope and conger eels in rough ground. Wire varies in quality; some of the 'stainless' is in fact quick to rust, and will deteriorate under the plastic sleeving so that corrosion remains hidden until the wire snaps.

Wire cannot be joined or knotted by standard methods. Light wire is attached with a simple hitch, then twisted back on itself and the sleeving fused with the flame of a match. Heavy wire is secured with special crimped sleeves fixed with a pair of crimping pliers.

Floats

Shop floats are made from balsa wood or plastic and sold in a vast range of shapes and sizes. Standard seafishing floats buoy up between ½ and 2 oz (15 and 55 g). They are expensive, and if losses are inevitable it makes sense to use home-made substitutes. Anything that floats and can be attached to the line will do. Heavy floats are a complete waste of money, because nothing rivals an ordinary toy balloon inflated to about 3 in (7.5 cm) in diameter. Coloration is unimportant. It helps to paint floats both black and a bright colour. Yellow and orange stand out against dull sea, but in foam and against the light black is far more conspicuous.

Bits and pieces

My tackle bag contains beads which are used to prevent split rings from sliding too far, scraps of cork and foam for floats, silver-paper attractors, and lots of assorted oddments like rubber bands and feathers. Every angler needs a good selection of rubbish, for from rubbish springs forth ingenuity and better fishing.

KNOTS FOR SHOREFISHING

There are scores of different knots. Many are complicated works of art that date back to the days of flax and silk lines. We need know about three, which are easily tied, reliable and of high strength—about 90 per cent that of the actual line. Absolute familiarity with each knot is essential because you will have to tie them in the dark and with fingers numbed by frost. All the knots described are variations on a theme; once the principle is grasped, you will be able to tie them blindfold. Given that the knots are well formed, the only precaution necessary is to leave about ⅛ in (3 mm) of free nylon on the loose ends to allow for stretching. Knots pull together better if the nylon is lubricated by saliva.

Tucked half-blood knot

A very tough knot used to secure hooks, swivels and split rings (fig 15). It is never used directly on sinkers, though, but always with a link of some kind, preferably a split ring. Three to five turns are plenty, and it is important to give the final tuck or the knot will be much weakened.

Fig 15   Tucked half-blood knot

For joining swivels, hooks, lures and split-rings to nylon line

Double-blood knot

The standard knot for joining two pieces of nylon whose diameters differ by less than 25 per cent (fig 16). Three to five turns are adequate; too many make the knot too bulky and might even prevent it from tightening.

Stand-off knot

The loop formed by this is the foundation of the paternoster rig, and does away with the need for wire spreaders should you consider them

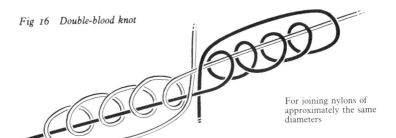

Fig 16   Double-blood knot

For joining nylons of approximately the same diameters

unnecessary (fig 17). Five or more turns give sufficient stiffness to hold the loop clear of the main line. The knot may be further stiffened by sleeving the loop with a 1 in (2.5 cm) length of plastic tubing. Empty ballpoint refills are ideal. If short hook links are required, tie a big loop, then cut it to form a loose end for hook attachment.

Elastic band stop knot

Perhaps knot is the wrong description of this simple hitch (fig 19). A 1 in (2.5 cm) length of band is clove-hitched to the line; or the line is hitched to the band. It makes no difference: a blob is formed to arrest the float.

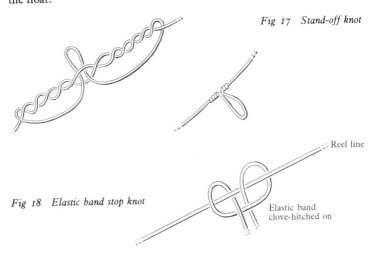

Fig 17   Stand-off knot

Reel line

Fig 18   Elastic band stop knot

Elastic band clove-hitched on

5 *Casting*

A series of books could be written on casting; certainly it is impossible to describe every method in a single chapter. A detailed analysis of all the many ways in which rod and reel may be used to propel a sinker is hardly relevant in a simple guide to fishing such as this is. I have chosen to describe one simple cast that throws baits and sinkers up to 150 yds (140 m), and which may be used almost anywhere. The style is a mixture of the South African and layback casts, requires basic tackle only, and is learned in a few hours. Better progress is made if the beginner surrenders himself to a professional coach from the very start, but as such guidance is not generally available in Britain, the alternative is to study from pictures and text, then learn by trial and error. It is easier if two casters work together so that one may criticise the other.

The secret of casting is rhythm. Establishing a comfortable swing of rod and body is absolutely essential. Throughout the early stages of learning to cast, the beginner must concentrate on style and timing; actual casting distance is irrelevant. Unless the action is so deeply imprinted that the cast becomes automatic, it is impossible to make the best progress. Long distance is the product of good style. The fisherman who paces out all his practice casts, be they long or short, is doomed to failure. Watch any good caster in action and you see that he pays the same attention to detail whether lobbing 50 yds (45 m) or blasting out 150 yds (140 m). In fact, excellent casters are a disappointment to watch. The rod swings in an easy arc and flicks straight, almost lazily it appears. The only evidence of the colossal power is the screaming reel and the giant arch of line drifting in the sunlight.

BODY SWING AND ARM MOVEMENT

In the same way that a golfer spends hours perfecting his drive, the caster must work at the power stroke until it is second nature to him. For practising there is no need for reel, sinker and line. In fact, the rod itself may be replaced by a piece of stick. Work on the stroke until it becomes a really powerful flick where body and arms act in perfect unison. Diagrams showing the sequence (figs 19 a–e and 20 a–b) appear below in the section on casting sequence (pp. 57–62).

26 *Suffolk angler Roy Cook hurls out 120 yd (110 m) with his casting pole. An adaptation of the original pole and line used for centuries, the casting pole used by Cook demonstrates quite clearly that long rods and sophisticated reels are unnecessary for long distance casting.*

Starting position

1. Imagine a line out to sea in the direction of the cast. Stand with your toes on the line and feet comfortably apart. Shoulders must be parallel to the line.
2. Grip the rod with hands shoulder width apart.
3. Hold the rod parallel to your chest, about 1 ft (30 cm) away, and sloping down to the right at about 30 degrees. The left hand is at eye level.
4. Maintaining arm and rod position, swing waist and shoulders 45 degrees to the right. Bending at the waist and right knee, lean away from the casting direction until the shoulders have dipped through about 1 ft (30 cm).
Practise getting into the starting position until it is familiar.

Swing

5. The first phase of the power stroke is a direct reversal of the positioning movement already described. Swing the shoulders back parallel to the cast line, straighten the right leg and the body at the waist. The arms must not alter their position relative to the shoulders. Look at the left hand all the time.
Practise the swing until it becomes smooth and fast.

Punch

6. As the shoulders swing back parallel to the cast line, do not stop, but continue until the chest faces almost straight down the cast line. As the shoulders pass through parallel, pull the left hand forwards and upwards, then down to the bottom left of the ribcage. At the same time punch the right hand forwards and upwards as if hurling a javelin. After the swing, pull and punch, **Stop dead**. There is no follow-through on a cast other than to release the line. You do not follow through with a body action of any description. All through the action, concentrate on the left hand: watch it rise, then pull down. As the hand flashes towards the ribs, switch focus out to sea. From the very start, movements of shoulders, waist and arms all flow together. There is no one–two action, but a single sweep.

    By concentrating on the left hand throughout, you ensure that the shoulders and waist play their part; the initial 30 degree rod slope eliminates the overhead cast. Practise the whole sequence until you can hit the rod very hard indeed, but under complete control.

    The action depends upon the shoulders and waist building up rod speed so that the final punch is applied to a moving sinker. Exactly how you interpret the sequence and modify it for your own preference and physique is unimportant so long as the basic principles are retained. One obvious modification is stance. As you swing through and really slam the rod, balance shifts. The faster the action and greater the load, the more you wobble. Maximum power occurs as the arms react, and

27 Off-the-ground cast (1): measuring the leader drop between sinker and rod tip. The length to suit the caster and his tackle is found by experiment, but thereafter the drop remains constant.

28 Off-the-ground cast (2): the sinker and line are laid out on the beach, the reel is out of gear and the caster settles into the starting position. Note the height of the left hand, and the rod tip position close to the beach but not touching it.

29 Off-the-ground cast (3): the swing through and punch/pull. The sinker lifts off the beach and accelerates quickly but smoothly to full speed. For a detailed explanation of this power stroke, see the expanded sequence of close-up photographs.

30 Off-the-ground cast (4): the line is released and the sinker flies out to sea. Aim to cast high, and point the rod tip so that the line flows straight out of the tip ring. Stop the line as soon as the sinker splashes down.

therefore the stance should be adjusted so that you are absolutely firm at that point. Most anglers find it useful to move the left foot 6 in (15 cm) back from the line of cast, and turn the toes more in the casting direction.

TACKLE ASSEMBLY FOR CASTING PRACTICE

Learn to cast with sinkers of 4–6 oz (115–170 g). Light weights are difficult to time; heavy ones are too much of a strain until your muscles have hardened to the strange movements. Set the reel on the rod at shoulder width, or mount it low and control it with the left hand. It is far easier to learn with a fixed-spool because there are fewer things to go wrong. If you insist on a multiplier, load with no more than 100 yds (90 m) of line and tighten the casting control. Always use a strong casting leader and attach the sinker via split ring, never directly to nylon.

CASTING SEQUENCE

Off-the-ground cast

1. Position your feet on the cast line. Hold the rod almost vertically and release line until the sinker hangs halfway down the rod. Note the position exactly: line up the sinker tip with a ring or the spigot (fig 19a). Flip the reel out of gear, or open the bale arm.

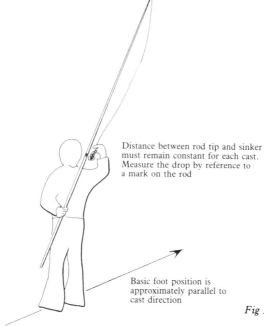

Distance between rod tip and sinker must remain constant for each cast. Measure the drop by reference to a mark on the rod

Basic foot position is approximately parallel to cast direction

Fig 19a

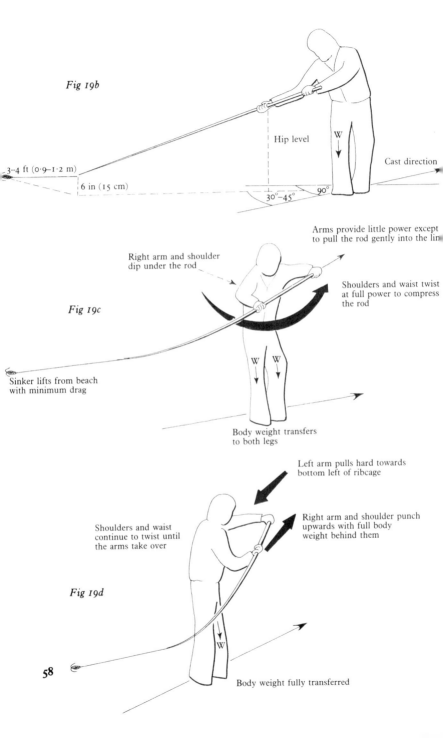

Fig 19b

3–4 ft (0·9–1·2 m)

6 in (15 cm)

Hip level

W

Cast direction

30°–45°   90°

Arms provide little power except to pull the rod gently into the line

Right arm and shoulder dip under the rod

Shoulders and waist twist at full power to compress the rod

Fig 19c

Sinker lifts from beach with minimum drag

W   W

Body weight transfers to both legs

Left arm pulls hard towards bottom left of ribcage

Right arm and shoulder punch upwards with full body weight behind them

Shoulders and waist continue to twist until the arms take over

Fig 19d

W

58

Body weight fully transferred

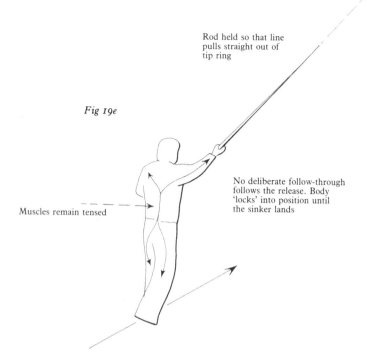

Rod held so that line pulls straight out of tip ring

Fig 19e

No deliberate follow-through follows the release. Body 'locks' into position until the sinker lands

Muscles remain tensed

2. Turn towards the starting position but before settling swing the sinker away so that it lies on the ground with the leader at right angles to the cast line and the leader tight between rod and sinker.
3. Settle into the starting position. Viewed from above, the rod lies at about 30 degrees to the cast line (fig 19b). The rod tip is close to the ground but not touching.
4. **Swing through** (fig 19c).
5. **Punch**, and release the line (fig 19d).
6. As the sinker flies, hold the rod so that line pulls straight out from the tip ring (fig 19e).
7. Stop the line as soon as the sinker lands.

The cast really is that simple. Work at it, feeling for the rhythm. Forget distance and concentrate on smoothness and correct timing. In no time the sinker flies much farther than you thought possible. 130 yds (120 m) is quite easy and should be achieved within a couple of weeks.

Fishing cast

Off-the-ground casting is fine for open beaches where you fish from hard ground. Even spiked sinkers lift off without catching. But as soon as you fish surf or rocks, the style is useless. However, having mastered

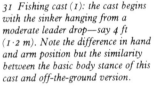

31 *Fishing cast (1): the cast begins with the sinker hanging from a moderate leader drop—say 4 ft (1·2 m). Note the difference in hand and arm position but the similarity between the basic body stance of this cast and off-the-ground version.*

32 *Fishing cast (2): swing the sinker in the 'one . . . two . . . three . . . four' pattern explained in the text. Use the minimum power necessary to move the sinker in its arc; if there should be any loss of rhythm, stop the sinker and start again.*

33 *Fishing cast (3): as you anticipate count 'four', the sinker reaches its highest point on the inswing and the cast begins with a body twist. The cast movement then follows the off-the-ground style. Note that the left hand has risen and is at eye level.*

the basic cast you are in the happy position of knowing how to cast well, and any change in technique can be undertaken with absolute confidence.

To overcome the drawbacks of the ground cast, we need only begin the action with the sinker in midair, thus disregarding the roughness of the beach or, within reason, depth of surf. The original layback cast hangs a sinker on a short leader directly beneath the rod tip. It takes a lot of rod arc to get it moving and some of the cast's power is wasted. Swinging the sinker back and forth generates inertia and positions the sinker so that every bit of the action is utilised.

1. Hang the sinker from a 4 ft (1.2 m) leader drop.
2. Settle into a comfortable starting position, but lower the left hand so that the rod slopes *upwards* 30 degrees. The plan view remains unaltered at 30 degrees to the line of cast.
3. Swing the sinker backwards and forwards in an arc parallel to the cast line, or slightly more towards you (fig 20a). Use the minimum rod movement that keeps the pendulum going. Practise until the swing is smooth and almost automatic.
4. Now introduce a rhythm similar to this: begin with the sinker stationary, swing away, back in so the leader is parallel to the ground, out again, then in. Count it aloud: 'one ... and ... two ... and ... three ... and ... four'. If anything goes wrong, stop and begin again. **Never** keep on with the swing in the hope that it will correct itself. It never does.
5. The cast proper begins with the sinker reaching maximum height on the inswing, that is, on the count of 'four'. But if you wait until it reaches that point, the slight delay while your nervous system transmits the cast message to your body will cause you to miss and the leader goes

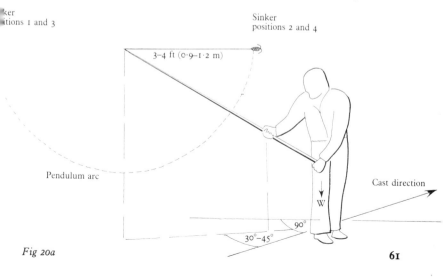

ker
tions 1 and 3

Sinker
positions 2 and 4

3–4 ft (0.9–1.2 m)

Pendulum arc

Cast direction

W

90°

30°–45°

Fig 20a

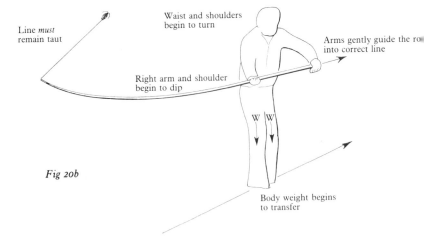

Line *must* remain taut

Waist and shoulders begin to turn

Arms gently guide the rod into correct line

Right arm and shoulder begin to dip

W W

Fig 20b

Body weight begins to transfer

slack. Instead, count 'one ... and ... two ... and ... three ... and ...'; then, as you come to the 'f' of 'four', start to cast. Your rod will whip up the sinker right on time.

6. **Swing,** but this time your left hand is low to begin with and must be swept up to eye level (fig 20 b). Do it smoothly; there is no rush. The sinker will not hit the ground if the swing and beginning are properly timed.

7. **Punch.** Release the reel line.

8. Watch the sinker in flight, and stop the line as it touches the ground.

With sinker alone, the average man should be able to cast 160 yds (150 m) and the practical fishing range will be comfortably over 120 yds (10 m). In fact, the style is so good that it takes a conscious effort to throw under 100 yds (90 m), which means that overcasting is possible. Just because you cast well there is no sense in always blasting out the sinker. Many times the fish are right inshore; sometimes literally underfoot in the surf. The sign of an immature fisherman is constantly striving for distance. More than a few anglers turn each fishing trip into their own casting tournament where they endeavour to outcast everyone else on the beach. The hallmark of a good angler is that his casting skill is a tool, not used indiscriminately or to impress others. He casts where the fish shoal and it is of no importance whether they are 10 or 110 yds away. The same easy cast drops the baits at his feet or jets them way out.

RODS

The only way the body can direct all its power to the sinker is with the correct style and the right tackle. As soon as the angler begins to feel the rhythm of the new cast, he can start to examine his tackle. The

major criteria for rod selection have already been discussed but it does no harm to recap on the major points: the rod should be fairly short, powerful enough to handle the sinker, yet still fully flexible. The action is really a matter of personal preference, but it is as well to begin with a medium-fast taper. The handle must be correct for the individual's physique.

Never tolerate too long a handle. The distance between the hands is quite critical, especially with the larger sinkers. If you cannot handle the rod with your hands in their correct positions on the handle, it is too long. Few anglers can master a rod more than 12 ft (3.7 m) long, and most would be better casters with shorter blanks. The difference between the theoretical maximum fishing distances of 10 and 15 ft (3 and 4.5 m) rods is marginal. If you need to shorten the rod, attack the butt. Should the handle then be too short, strip off the fittings and rebuild the complete butt section.

Shortening the rod will throw the ring spacings out of step. Thread the line up the rings and anchor it to a post. Pull on the rod and check the run of the line: if it follows the blank without being obviously over-ringed, it is satisfactory. Big gaps need filling in with more rings. In particular, watch the butt ring to make sure the line does not dive down into it from the reel side. It must flow through without touching. If the butt has been shortened, the ring will almost certainly need to be repositioned, and the rest of the rings moved up to compensate.

REELS

There is nothing to choose between the maximum casts of fixed-spools and multipliers. Use the reel you prefer. Fixed-spool reels must be kept filled with line or friction reduces the cast distance. It is very important to lock the drag nut before casting, or the spool rotates under pressure. It is even more important to slacken it afterwards because when a big fish hits the bait the clutch must be ready to react. Few anglers can hold down the line for really hard casting because the nylon cuts into the finger. A casting release device shifts all the pressure from the fingers to the rod and you can cast as hard as you like with no risk at all. Very hard casting introduces another problem though: the bale arm closes in midcast. Some reels are fitted with anti-inertia devices which prevent the bale arm from triggering too soon, but on many models you have to resort to clipping back the arm with an elastic band. Before opening the bale arm on either type of reel, turn the spool so that it is at the farthest-forward point of its travel, and then the line will not catch in the bale arm housing and flyer. Another point to watch is line tension: if the line is too slack on the spool it will cut into itself and tangle. Very loose line on a well filled spool tends to spring off, which is very troublesome if the line is twisted to begin with. The most beautiful tangles may occur.

Multiplier reels are trouble-free once mastered, but the learning stage is a nightmare unless you adopt a special approach. Never fill the reel with line; and oil it with very thick motor gear oil or even grease. Keep all the brake blocks in and tighten down the cast controller. To begin

34 Starting position (1): this is the start of the off-the-ground cast. Note the arm, shoulder and basic body positions and the rod angle, then refer to the text.

35 Starting position (2): the start of the fishing cast with the sinker swing. Note the difference between the basic stance and that of the off-the-ground style. See the text for explanation.

with, 100 yds (90 m) of line is more than enough. As your casting improves, slacken the brake progressively until you can cast all the line without any fear of an overrun. Tie on an extra 25 yds (or 25 m) of line at the base of the existing line, reset the cast controls to maximum and begin again, when all 125 yds (115 m) comes off with minimum braking, add more line, and so on until there comes a time when you cannot get the reel to run properly with its line load. Then take off the last piece of additional line. The reel should then contain the maximum length of line that you can properly control. Paint a dot on the spool flange to coincide with that amount, strip off all the knotted line and refill with new nylon.

The first casts with the new line must be carefully controlled by increasing the drag once again. Cast gently a few times, then boost the power at the same time releasing the control. This running-in procedure ensures that the line lies properly on the spool. Unless it is carried out, the nylon is likely to tangle within the first two or three casts. Avoid knots in the first 100 yds (90 m) of the line at least. A knot tearing off in midcast is likely to tie itself around the butt ring and might even rip the ring from its mounting. The tangling occurs because the knot is much heavier than the rest of the line and flies from the reel at a different tangent. It shoots higher than the main line, then ducks down into the butt ring with disastrous consequences. The same thing happens with incorrectly tied leader knots.

Fine control of the spool, casting smoothness and mechanical clatter are the province of the reel lubricants. Plain bearings and ballraces must be well oiled if they are to work properly and last a long time. The pressures and friction created by a hard cast are truly enormous: it is not unknown for a tournament reel to smoke and literally scorch. Fishing reels suffer less, but attention to lubrication will extend their lives. 90 grade gear oil is good for most reels, stays in the bearings and smooths the cast. Greater control and improved performance of worn reels demand a thicker oil. STP oil additive is excellent; if a little too viscous for routine use, it may be thinned with ordinary engine oil.

Most reels cast best with 175–225 yds (160–205 m) of line. Large reels used for tope and other fast-running species must be filled to capacity even if they are difficult to control that way. Tope are often hooked at close range, so the casting performance might be of little importance anyway. Screw down the controls and cast as smoothly as you can. Never take off line to make life easier: a good tope will take every yard you can cram on to the spool.

SINKER WEIGHT FOR MAXIMUM DISTANCE

In practice sessions, without the hindrance of traces and baits, there is little to choose between the maximum casting distances of sinkers of various sizes. If the tackle is matched to the sinker, the longest casts with weights between 2 and 8 oz (55 and 225 g) vary by no more than 40 yds (35 m) or so, and most anglers find they cast farthest with 4 oz (115 g). On the beach, where big baits and headwinds often complicate

36 *Swing and punch (1): as the sinker reaches maximum height on the inswing of the fishing cast, the body begins to twist and the left arm rises. The right arm and shoulder dip under the rod.*

37 *Swing and punch (2): the shoulders and waist have twisted as hard as possible and the left arm is pulled high and away from the body. The right shoulder and hand are under the rod for maximum leverage and the longest arc of movement. In this position the caster is ready to make the final punch.*

38 *Swing and punch (3): the punch that drives the sinker to maximum velocity. The right arm punches forwards and upwards as hard as possible. The left arm is poised to strike; in fact the two movements follow within a split second of each other, but for absolute smoothness you should get the impression that the right arm starts off just ahead.*

39 *Swing and punch (4): the left hand pulls down as the right reaches full power. The sinker is almost at full speed and the rod is doubled over into its full curve. The release comes a split second later; exact timing is a matter of trial and error, although most casters seem to release automatically at the right moment.*

40 Swing and punch (5): the sinker is on its way. The rod is pointed up the line and the caster's thumb hovers over the spool to iron out any loose coils of line should they rise from the reel.

casting, the bigger sinkers fly farther; indeed, the lighter weights might literally stop in midair. Losses are most apparent with 2 and 3 oz (55 and 85 g), marked with 4 oz (115 g), and much reduced by the big 6 and 8 oz (170 and 225 g) weights, which cut through all but the fiercest wind.

Using big weights in rough weather is common sense, and has nothing at all to do with sportsmanship. The assertion that all heavy tackle is unnecessary does not stand up in everyday shorefishing. The light tackle advocates have their point: lighter tackle makes ordinary fishing more fun. But there are times when you either fish heavy or catch nothing, simply because your sinkers and baits cannot fly far enough or anchor in the swells. Normally, 4 and 6 oz (115 and 170 g) are enough to deal with all but the extremes of fishing. Yet even the difference between 4 and 6 oz is important at times.

A 4 oz (115 g) sinker casts easily and pulls baits through most winds. It anchors well in fairly fast tides, yet the line pressure upon retrieve is low enough to insure against spool damage even if collapsible gripwires are not used. The bigger 6 oz (170 g) sinker is a real advantage in gales or where the tide runs fast. It does have great disadvantages, though: the line pressure on retrieving might overpower the reel's gearing, or smash the spool; and many anglers cannot cast the sinker because it is too much for their long rods and physique. The answer is to use a 5 oz (140 g) sinker.

A 5 oz (140 g) sinker flies slowly and with the dragging power necessary to pull baits into gales, holds bottom against the strongest tides, but is still easy to cast—almost as easy as a 4 oz (115 g) one. For some reason the weight is missed from the standard range, which jumps from 4 to 6 oz (115 to 170 g) with nothing in between to iron out the enormous step—it is in fact 50 per cent. As more anglers demand the weight, lead sinker manufacturers are moulding them, but some areas continue with the traditional range. There are places where you cannot buy a 5 oz sinker, and the tackle dealer looks at you strangely if you even ask him for one. The answer, naturally, is mould your own; it is far cheaper anyway. In trials without baits, most anglers are surprised to discover that they cast farthest of all with the sinker. A further advantage is that the weight replaces both 4 and 6 oz for most fishing. The majority of British shorecasting needs 3 and 5 oz (85 and 140 g) sinkers only; the saving of space in tackle boxes alone justifies the expense of a new mould, should that be necessary.

41 A firm grip on the spool is absolutely essential. The leader knot is tucked to one side of the spool so that it cannot cut into the caster's thumb.

LEARNING TO CAST

The easiest way to learn any skill is under the guidance of a qualified instructor. The golf professional and tennis coach are vital to their respective sports: the beginner who is keen to advance beyond the basics automatically seeks their counsel. But except in gamefishing, the professional coach plays little part in the angling world. This is absurd, because the time, money and frustration saved by a few hours' teaching is enormous. Learning to cast is easy when there is an expert beside you to point out and correct faults almost before they develop, and certainly before they become second nature. Progress will be rapid: three hours will see the sinker flying over 100 yds (90 m) even if the angler has never cast before. Ninety per cent of British beach anglers are poor casters who never had a moment's instruction.

Constant practice is not essential for good casting performance. In one hour, once a week, the caster who practises intelligently will improve by many yards. If to begin with he throws 80 yds (70 m), one year's work—a total of less than 50 hours, say—should double his range, after which 1 hour a month will maintain the level.

Tournament tackle is never essential for shorefishing, but is fun to use in practice once the caster is reasonably competent. Casting for its own sake is a great sport, and if you are working over grass, why not make the best of your opportunity to throw the sinker as far as you can? But never confuse the objectives of the two forms of the sport; use fishing tackle on the beach because it is the tool of the trade.

SAFETY

A speeding sinker is lethal. If the line snaps in midcast, there is no control of the sinker in either distance or direction. Worst are the tournament pendulum casts where for a fraction of a second the sinker is swung very hard through an arc along the beach. If the line snaps then—and often it does—the sinker hurtles towards bystanders. There have been accidents, fortunately rather minor but still requiring surgery. Never underestimate the power of a flying sinker: a snap-off may travel over 400 yds (350 m); at 200 yds (180 m), a 6 oz (170 g) sinker will smash through a tiled roof; at 20 yds (18 m), it will slice through an oil drum.

The burden of responsibility for the safety of people, animals and property rests upon the caster. Those who practise in fields and parks are duty bound to make certain there is enough space. At least 500 yds (450 m) is the minimum in the casting direction. The flying sinker is the obvious danger, but loose line is a menace, especially in fields where livestock grazes. Many farm animals have required veterinary attention after eating discarded lines; some have died from obstructed intestines. Loose line must be found and taken home to be burned. A useful way to locate lost line is to walk with the sun in your eyes, which makes the coils shine like beacons.

6 *Legering and general techniques*

Most seafishes are caught on or close to the seabed. Unless baits are to be floated or spun in midwater, legering is one of the best methods of hooking shoreline species; it is so effective that many anglers use it to the exclusion of everything else, a shortsighted attitude perhaps but a tribute to the leger's effectiveness. It is useful from open beach, harbour and estuary. You can fish a tiny ragworm for flounders in a creek, or anchor a bunch of lugworms in the maelstrom of a winter cod sea.

INCREASING THE ATTRACTION OF LEGER TACKLE

The primary attraction of leger tackle is the bait. In cloudy water the oils and juices from the bait drift along on the tide to lay a scent trail, which hunting fishes trace to its source. It matters little if the baits lie on the seabed or wave in the current just above. Nor is visual attraction important, because many of the fishes that respond to legered natural baits locate them by scent and smell, and can swallow the hook without seeing the bait at all. In clear water over sand and shingle it might help if the baits flash in the sunlight or move along the seabed. Jerking the baits certainly attracts flounders and other flatfishes, and might encourage a more determined bite from many other species too. On shallow sands offshore from a surfstrand, slow tackle retrieve prevents baits and line from sinking into the bottom. The speed at which the surge of the water normally drives them into the sand is amazing: half a minute might see the sinker, bait and many yards of line buried out of sight. Some fishes can locate sunken baits, but many ignore them or circle the area in apparent confusion.

WHERE TO STAND FOR BETTER CASTING

Standing in the wrong place to cast will slash distances. On moderately sloping beaches and from harbour walls and piers it is sufficient to stand reasonably near the water's edge, or as close as obstructions and swells permit. Very deep beaches are better fished by standing well away from the sea. Steep banks of shingle which shelve down to the sea in a series of steps can be dangerous should the breakers sweep in. Casting from halfway down a step is difficult because shingle to the caster's rear fouls the rod tip. Move back up to the next highest platform and cast from there. The distance lost is more than regained by the extra casting power possible from firm ground.

Surfbeaches are almost the opposite: the shore slopes so gently that high- and low-water marks might be half a mile (800 m) apart. Even at the top of a spring tide the water might be no more than 3 ft (0.9m) deep. Unless the fishes are very close inshore, fishing at the water's edge is unprofitable. Wading is the answer; but too many anglers put on chest-high boots and wade too far and too deep. You can wade so far in long boots that the water-tables sweep in and lift you off your feet. Sometimes that is very dangerous, and always it prevents good casting because your arms and tackle would need to begin from underwater. Back in the shallows where water swirls around your thighs, casting is easy. As on steep beaches, the distance lost is more than compensated for by extra casting range. If you want to wade deep, go dressed for swimming, for swim you will.

CASTING TRAJECTORY

Very few anglers vary the trajectory of their casts to suit winds. In normal fishing, the sinker climbs to the right height almost automatically and there is no need to control it. Every angler naturally casts to a certain angle and unless it is obviously excessively high or low, distance is not cut. But winds play havoc with casting and it is essential to match the sinker trajectory to them. Tailwinds give enormous lift, which is exploited by casting higher and letting the reel run more freely than normal. Headwinds and casting do not mix: the reel overruns and the sinker almost stops in the air. Increase sinker weight and cast low, sometimes so low that the tackle skims the waves. Brake the reel with the cast controls and help it even further by dabbing at the spool with the thumb if any loose coils start to come off. Crosswinds are mastered with a normal or slightly low cast combined with a freely running reel. The line drifts downwind in a giant loop, and instead of the normal 120 yds (110 m), a 100 yds (90 m) cast strips off up to 160 yds (145 m) of line. Do nothing to stop the loop billowing unless the loose line risks snagging on nearby groynes and breakwaters. Just let it go, then, once the sinker is in the water, reel it back as soon as possible.

DEEP WATER AND LONG-RANGE CASTING

If you cast into deep water and stop the reel as soon as the sinker splashes down, the tackle will sink back through an arc to land almost under your feet. A 100 yds cast, say, might settle less than 50 yds out. Maintain distance by letting go more line. Fishing with a fixed-spool reel is easier because you do not need to stop the line when the sinker lands, but multipliers must be braked then allowed to run again or the line will tangle. Allow the line to run off for anything up to 30 seconds—you can tell when the sinker is on the bottom by the sudden line slackness. The line itself continues to sink long after the sinker has settled and you have to wind back the slack progressively. This is important over rough ground where loose line sinks and tangles in the inshore kelp: more about that later, in the section on weeds and rubbish (p. 81).

HOLDING AGAINST THE TIDE

Gripwired sinkers are used for routine legering in fast water. Unless the tide is really fierce, you cast out, then either hold the rod or place it in a rest. Very fast water, common on cod and whiting beaches, needs a modified technique, or the traces sweep ashore again. Cast out, then let at least 25 yds (or 25 m) more line run off into the tide. Set the reel in gear, prop the rod in its rest and watch the line. If it tightens and settles, leave it alone. Should it sweep round in the tide, flicking alternately tight and slack, the wires are bouncing along the seabed. Try letting go more line, but if that fails too, wind in and begin again. In most cases the sinker will anchor because the great arc of line alters the angle of pressure and also gives a few moments' grace for the sinker to dig in before the line initially tightens. One disadvantage is that the tackle settles up to 30 yds (25 m) downtide of your fishing place. Correct that by walking that distance up the beach before casting out, then return to base once the sinker is out there.

42 For trouble-free casting with multiplier reels it is absolutely essential that the line is wound on evenly and under constant tension. Pieces of weed, lumps and tight patches will create havoc.

ROD RESTS

The rod rest is a necessary evil. Desirable though holding the rod may be, it is physically impossible to hold a rod against fierce tide pressure for more than a few minutes. A 100 yds (90 m) length of line stretched across a racing spring ebb doubles the rod and makes the nylon whistle. A firm rest is therefore essential. A rod held vertically keeps line above the inshore breakers and signals bites clearly, but does exaggerate wind movement. Some rods blow about so much that you cannot tell a bite. If that happens, lean the rod at a shallower angle and incline it away from the sea so that the rod lies with the wind.

BITE DETECTION

The most sensitive bite detector is the handline, because every tug is transmitted to the angler's fingertips. By holding the rod and looping nylon over the fingers of the reel hand, the fisherman creates much the same situation : direct contact between himself and the hook. Bites are positive; even gentle sucks and trembles are clear. If anything the system is too sensitive, and inexperienced anglers strike too soon. Some species feed slowly and the initial mouthings of the bait must not trigger a strike: conger eels sometimes play with the bait for fifteen minutes before making off. Wait and see what happens. For every fish hit too late a dozen have the hook snatched out of their mouth.

Flickering of the rod tip is the classic bite indication. With the rod upright in its rest, any movement is readily visible. Again, the tendency is towards striking too early. Wind, tide and weeds pluck at the line to cause false bites. Fishing rough seas, it is essential to study the rod tip for several minutes to establish the natural rhythm; bites then appear as a break in the normal pattern. In calm water, especially when fishing for running species like tope, throw the reel out of gear and engage the clicker. Bite indication is visual, plus the audible warning that line is running off the reel. Water movement snatching the line also trips the clicker; fast tides rip it off and the method is useless unless the reel is set in gear with the clutch tightened sufficiently to cancel out the pressure. Setting the clutch obviously makes the system less sensitive, but is useful especially at night. Free spool and clicker can be used with a hand-held rod. With shy species you let the line run off so they feel no tension while investigating the bait.

Very hard tides require a different system where, instead of bending the rod, the fish flicks it straight. The anchored sinker maintains line tension until a fish strikes. The momentum of its attack snatches the wires out of the seabed and the trace and line drift free in the current. The rod springs upright in its rest and you wind in the slack as quickly as possible. In many ways this bite is best of them all: it is absolutely positive, and nine times out of ten the fish is firmly hooked.

43 *Stormy seas and masses of floating weed—the shorefisherman's nightmare.*

BITES AND STRIKING

Bites might be anything from a tremor that you sense rather than positively feel to a full-blooded wallop with the rod torn from its rest. The assertion that you can tell the species by its bite is largely false. Congers, pollack and wrasse sometimes take the bait in such a manner as to suggest their identity, but fishes in general bite according to tide strength, light intensity, and other obscure factors. You find they may well bite harder at night, in rough seas and according to shoal size. Competition for available food ensures that species like cod, mackerel and whiting snatch their prey. There are few rules about bites; nor does their ferocity reflect the size of the fish. Some of the big specimens bite very gently, yet a tiny pouting almost drags the rod out to sea. A fisherman's response to bites is based on experience. There is no way to describe a bite: you have to feel it to know it. Reactions to bites also vary, and again, only familiarity tells you whether to react or to wait. But if in doubt, wait a little longer.

Striking a bite is one of shorefishing's pantomime turns. Some men run backwards; others beat the rod as if it were a conductor's baton. Striking in the accepted sense is a waste of time at long range. The effect of the most enormous rod swipe is muted to nothing by even 100 yds (90 m) of nylon line. The way to keep up pressure is to reel in and perhaps walk slowly backwards to maintain tension. Whatever you do must be exaggerated, but not made farcical. Galloping through the surf looks impressive—unless you fall over—but does no good except as a ego-inflator. By the time you strike, the fish is most likely either hooked or long gone. Only occasionally does the strike actually drive home the hook.

Bite detection is a reaction; the bite itself occurred a split second earlier and the hook is now either in the fish's jaws or lying on the seabed again. The force with which the fish hits a bait is at least ten times as hard as it appears. As an experiment run off 100 yds (90 m) of line, then tug on the end to see how far you can move the rod tip. Results confirm that when a fish moves the tip even a little bit, the trace was jerked considerably, perhaps enough to drive home the hookpoint with no other help necessary. If rods did not bend nor lines stretch, you could strike with greater effect, but even that would be effective only when the strike itself was timed to coincide with the fish's having tugged at the bait, or at least holding it in its jaws. The bite signalled by the rod tip or fingers is late: it takes time for the impulse to travel up the line. That delay, coupled to the angler's reaction time and subsequent transmission time of his strike, makes striking a hit-or-miss affair.

A far better method of increasing the numbers of fishes hooked is to rig the trace so that the fish hits against something solid. In practice, anchoring the bait and trace to a gripwired sinker improves the ratio of bites to successful hookings. A fish snatching the bait is brought up short by the sinker's inertia and the hook drives into its jaws. Even light, unwired sinkers have a certain amount of inertia, as indeed do traces buoyed up by a float—it takes a lot of pressure to sink a normal seafishing float. Of course, some fishes bite so gently that the hook just hangs in their mouth. Exactly how you overcome this is one of the problems of long-range seafishing.

Short-range striking can be effective. In freeline and light floatfishing for mullet, when you can see the fish sucking at the baits, a quick sharp strike will sink the hook. Yet again, for every fish you hook another escapes because you pulled the bait away too soon. Big fish like conger hooked at short range are more easily controlled by a powerful strike immediately followed by hard line tension to lift them away from the bottom. Let a conger get his tail around a rock and you have trouble. Hit him hard, jerk his head up and he has more chance of losing the battle.

PLAYING A FISH

Playing a fish is a game without rules. When the rod slams over you are on your own. If it is a very big fish your arms ache and rod pressure grinds the butt into your stomach. Your mind goes blank: what did they recommend you should do, those experts whose books made it all sound so simple? You fumble with the reel controls; line bunches and tangles, and you pick at it with trembling fingers. And all the time, the fish is out there: boring down into the deep water where there are rocks to snap the line; tearing across the shallows so fast that spray flies from the reel.

How to play the fish is something every angler must learn for himself. Everything you ever read or heard will be forgotten during the fight. But somehow, almost naturally it seems, you do react the right way. At first the fish has it all his own way. Then comes a stalemate when neither of you can beat the other. You gain line, then it goes again. Almost imperceptibly the balance tips towards you; line comes back on the reel and stays there. Now the fish is rolling on the surface or wallowing in the surf. You drive home the gaff or just grab it by the tail; then it is all over.

Stripped of emotion and drama, fighting a fish is a matter of exerting all the pressure the line can take, insuring against breakage by using the clutch, and gaining line when you can. If the tackle is properly matched and assembled, there is no reason to lose the fish except by carelessness and sheer bad luck. Having a tope strip all 150 yds (140 m) from the reel is your own fault: nobody should go toping with that amount of line. Ill luck is the rock that cuts your line, the breaker that sweeps the fish out to deep water just as you grab for it, the fish so powerful you cannot do anything with it.

Keep the line tight at all times: that is the golden rule. Rushing the fight is another very good way to get smashed. Time is on the angler's side. Every run and dive the fish makes tires the fish more than it tires you. You can transfer the strain to the tackle, but the fish has no allies. If it wants to run hundreds of yards, let it do so unless the ground is very rough. Try to anticipate its every move; use the clutch to iron out

44 *Long-range fishing in fast tides for cod and whiting is more comfortable with a rod rest. Bites are easily detected by movement of the rod tip.*

sudden and unexpected surges. Never use the reel as a winch, but pump in line by raising the rod, lowering it and at the same time winding in the slack, then raising it again. Take the line as it comes, never indulge in a direct tug of war. As long as some line remains on the spool, things are going fairly well. Most big fish are lost either very early in the fight when the hook straightens or pulls free, or in the last few yards. When it sees the angler or feels hard ground under its belly, a fish goes mad: in blind panic it swirls back to the sea. Let it go; then bring it back again. Most attempts to hold the fish result in a broken line or a straight hook. Let the fish drift ashore under minimum pressure; the line acts as a guide, never a towrope. From rocks, piers and harbour walls a dropnet, landing net or gaff are useful. Tailing is easier in the surf and from open beaches, especially for cod and tope. Bass and medium-weight fish need to be led ashore, then stranded by the receding waves.

45 Standing on the right part of the beach makes fishing easier. Had this angler waded right out into the surf he would not have been able to cast properly and might have been swept off his feet.

46 Very deep water between the mainland and an offshore rock. If the reel is stopped immediately after the sinker hits the water, the tackle will sink back inshore.

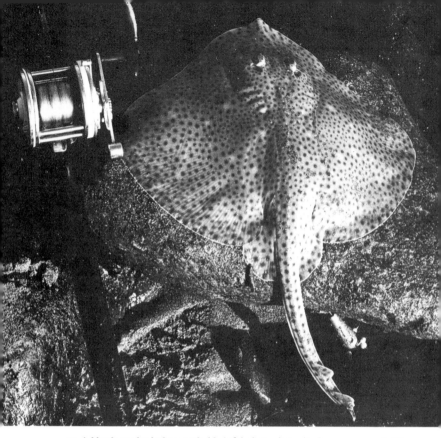

47 *A blonde ray hooked on sandeel bait fished on a leger rig. Legers are essential for fishes such as rays, which feed almost exclusively on the seabed.*

Some species need a different approach. Pollack and wrasse over rough ground take the bait and dive. You have to stop them before they get among the rocks. Very big fish take a lot of stopping—an excellent reason for not using very light tackle. Sometimes the line breaks, but you had no option but to try holding the fish back.

A conger gets its tail around a rock, and there is little to do about it except pull hard. You can try letting the line go slack in the hope that the fish will think it is free to return to open water again. Sometimes it works, sometimes not. Rays use their flat bodies to stick to the bottom by suction; in the tide they plane like huge kites. The greatest risk is that they may open their wings in the backwash with force enough to snap the line. But nothing in British inshore waters rivals tope. It is the nearest we have to a shorefisherman's gamefish. To hook one is to realise what fishing is all about.

AFTER PLAYING THE FISH

During the fight, line returns to the spool under great pressure. The tension alone can smash or distort a multiplier reel. Old bakelite spools actually explode out of the sideplates. The line is almost certainly badly spooled too—piled up on one side of the reel perhaps. Hard casting with the line in that state will result in a severe overrun that could snap the line. Gently lob the sinker about 50 yds (45 m), then rewind under normal tension. Cast about 100 yds (90 m), and then refill the spool correctly. Then check all the knots and traces, examine the nylon for fraying and replace whatever has been damaged in the fight. The tackle is then ready for hard casting once again.

WEEDS AND RUBBISH

Nothing is worse than floating weed. After a storm the inshore waters are a broth of seabelt, kelp and silky, stringy plant material of all descriptions. Sometimes fishing is impossible because the line is broken by the weight of the debris. The best thing is to go home: fishing is usually very bad then anyway. Occasional clumps are more of a nuisance: a bunch of wrack drags the line downtide so that for a moment you think there is a big fish on the hook. Nothing fights better

48 A centrifugal brake system fitted to a multiplier reel in order to make casting easier. All kinds of brakes are available, and they all work reasonably well. No caster can use a completely free-running multiplier that is not governed down in some way. Even the experts use brakes or special oils that slow the spool.

than a big plastic bag in a hard tide. If you hook a submerged floating tree trunk you will have just as much fun as with a giant tope. Landing rubbish is all part of shorefishing; sometimes it even brightens up your day.

Dragging weeds is hard on the spool, so pump the line back then relieve the pressure before recasting. Stripping off masses of weed is horrible, especially when your fingers are cold. It is easier to cut off the leader knot and slide the clumps off the free ends. Never let small beads of material build up in the line, because they destroy spool balance and also catch in the rings as the line flies out. Festooned traces need extra care: it is too easy to grab a handful of weed and find yourself impaled on the hook. On the other hand, it is most pleasant to clear the trace and find a fish underneath the rubbish. A big bunch of wrack can hide a respectable-sized fish.

7 Natural baits

Most fishermen catch nothing because they cast where there are no fish, and therefore baits make no difference to their chances. Where fishes are present and willing to feed, baits become vitally important because they are one of the few stimuli that might induce a fish to swallow the hook. Bad baits cancel out every effort you might have made to outwit your quarry.

Choice of baits is based on experience of species of fishes and their feeding habits. However, there are guidelines which at least suggest a basis for successful angling. The worm baits are universal and are the cornerstone of natural bait fishing. At least 50 per cent of all the seafish caught in Britain fall to lugworms or ragworms. Anglers abroad who fish with natural baits probably find that a high percentage of their fish are caught on worm baits; perhaps not on lugworms (*Arenicola marina*) or the species of *Nereis*, but on their indigenous equivalents. Worms are good baits for just about any species of fish, somewhere, sometimes.

Fish baits run a close second, and are superior for some fishing. In Britain, herrings and mackerel are popular and highly successful because they are the natural prey of the larger predators, being the intermediate link in the ecological chain. Herrings and mackerel are to sharks, rays and tope what bread and potatoes are to man.

The widespread use of fish and worms tends to overshadow other baits. Nearly everything that lives and grows on the seashore and in saltwater can be utilised as bait, sometimes very successfully. Many are seasonal and localised in distribution, and so will never become popular with the mass of anglers; but it is unwise to assume that because nearly everyone uses them, worms and the usual fish are naturally a better choice. On many occasions a shellfish, crab or tiny fish picked out from a tidepool proves best. The more baits there are in your repertoire, the less you depend on the traditional ones. Fishing is expanding, yet the capacity of our bait beds is static or falling. Bad weather and poor breeding seasons create shortages.

Collecting your own bait is best, but time and economics make worm digging in particular an unworkable proposition for many. A hundred lugworms cost £2 at the time of writing, which seems very expensive. But prices must be compared to the cost of digging your own. Most fishermen live miles away from the sea, and the better fishing places are not always near bait beds. An inland angler might be faced with a long journey before he actually sets off to go fishing. Tidal periods and fishing do not always coincide with digging hours; the pressures on bait

49 *Digging lugworms on a sandy beach where the worms are prolific ensures high-quality baits. But for many anglers it is impractical and too expensive to dig their own worms, and it is better to order supplies from the tackle dealer.*

beds are so intense that there is no guarantee of finding enough baits anyway. A lengthy round trip to dig over a patch of ground that fifty others have already excavated is time and money wasted. It makes more sense to order worms from a dealer.

Storage of livebait is a headache that has plagued anglers and dealers for years. Deepfreezing some species is impossible, and all forms of preservatives are taboo. Thousands of pounds' worth of bait are ruined every day, mostly because anglers cannot be bothered to look after it.

All baits must be cared for before, during and after fishing. Even the apparently tough baits like crabs and squid deteriorate rapidly. Direct sunlight, wind and all forms of heat and dryness ruin baits. Long-term storage in old wrappers, stale air and warmth rots them in no time at all. Ideally, every bait should be kept cool, damp and in darkness. A cooler box, with built-in icepacks, is an excellent investment, and can be used for both storage and carriage.

Fish are caught on all manner of things. The most unlikely offerings, such as cheese, banana and stale kipper, have been successful. Giant specimens were hooked on exotic scraps. It is silly to be swayed by these feats of angling. The capture of a few big fish is no reason to consider the routine use of strange baits; there is no such thing as a magic or secret bait. The majority of fish are caught on conventional, natural baits. The main consideration is freshness. Seafishermen spend huge sums on tackle, transportation, and gadgets, yet refuse to invest time and money in their baits. Until they do, catches will be poor, because nothing is worse than putrid chunks of herring or sun-dried scraps of lugworm. If that is all you have, do not bother to go fishing.

It is often said that big fish need big baits. There is some truth in this, but it is far from an inflexible rule. Baits which depend on smell for their attraction or need to be left in the water for long periods should be bigger. A whole side of mackerel sometimes proves more attractive than a sliver of flesh. If crabs and shrimps strip the hook within minutes of casting, or if small fish try to gorge the bait, stepping up the size ensures that some bait is in the water long enough to give a bigger fish a chance of finding it. As a rule, though, size should be more in line with the type of fishing. Baits for cod on the East Coast, where tides are fierce and the water extremely cloudy, must attract by smell, so size should be boosted to compensate for the speed at which the natural oils are washed away.

If you are short of bait, it pays to save it for the best stages of the tide: six good baits are better than a dozen scraps. By contrast, it would be wasting baits to fish whole sides of mackerel for average inshore pollack, which are perfectly satisfied with a sliver. Sometimes fish prefer different sizes as the mood takes them. One day surf bass tear into hooks loaded with worms and clams. Next time you need one tiny worm on a small hook in order to tempt a bite.

PRIMARY BAITS

Lugworms

Legered, drifted along the seabed or floatfished, lugworms are a good starting point for most seafishing and, if the fish are willing to feed, a substitute is seldom better. Lugworms are not used for the bigger predators.

SUPPLY

They are easy to dig on many sand, mud and grit beaches. Two methods are used: hunting out individual worms by locating both ends

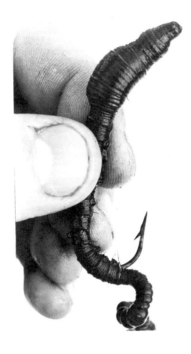

50 A lugworm, probably the most popular of all seafishing baits. Worms are mounted by threading the hook right down the middle of the body tube. If necessary, several should be mounted on the hook to make a bait of adequate size.

of the burrow; and trenching across a patch of ground dotted with casts. Most anglers prefer to buy worms because local bait beds are either too exploited or are uncovered at the wrong time to suit fishing hours. The size of lugworms varies from area to area. Norfolk and Suffolk worms are much smaller from those in the South-East. For some reason local worms often catch more fish than do imported lugworms.

CARE

Most worms are supplied whole and alive, wrapped in sheets of newspaper. The worms should be kept separated. Old paper must be changed, preferably every day. Keep the package cold and in the dark. Remove any dead or broken worms immediately or the whole batch will die. Some of the monster lugs are gutted and partially dried. They keep for months, and you can catch fish on them even when a mould develops.

LONG-TERM STORAGE

The inventor of a long-term system will become an instant millionaire. Deepfreezing does not work very well because the worms break up on thawing. Some anglers keep their baits in aquaria. No form of chemical preservative is allowable.

Thread worms on to the hook from head to tail, singly or in bunches. Long-shanked, fine wire hooks are less likely to burst the worms, but they are too flimsy for heavy work. Worms are used in combination with other baits, which either add to the attraction or make the worms go further. Squid and other tough baits help buffer the worms against heavy casting. Longer casts may be made by packing the worms close to the trace with a strip of water-soluble plastic (see the section on terminal rigs, p. 42).

Ragworms

A general bait for most pelagic and demersal species, ragworms are probably a more flexible bait than lugworms, and certainly more durable. The disadvantage is their limited distribution. The really huge 'king' ragworms are dug in only a few places such as Southend-on-Sea, Essex.

SUPPLY

Many shorelines and harbours support a population of one or more of the dozen or so species of British ragworms. Most are small red or white worms, though some are up to 6 in (15 cm) long, and the king ragworms are well over 1 ft (30 cm). Small baits may be dug easily enough, but the bigger ones are better bought from professional diggers.

CARE

Freshly dug worms are very fragile and need to toughen for a couple of

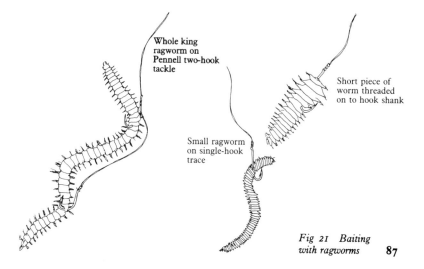

Whole king ragworm on Pennell two-hook tackle

Short piece of worm threaded on to hook shank

Small ragworm on single-hook trace

Fig 21 Baiting with ragworms **87**

51 *Deepfrozen whitebaits and brit. Fish baits of all kinds store for months in the freezer with no apparent deterioration. The only better fish baits are those freshly caught and used immediately afterwards.*

days before they are suitable for very hard casting. They may be kept wrapped in paper or covered in Vermiculite.

LONG-TERM STORAGE

Ragworms may be frozen, but they soften. They live for many weeks in aquaria or immersed in a stream of saltwater. The boxes and tanks must not be overcrowded; and lugworms and ragworms must never be mixed.

PRESENTATION

Thread on to the hook, head first (fig 21). Most ragworms fit nicely on to a long-shanked hook, but the bigger specimens are far too long. King ragworms can be broken into smaller segments or mounted on a two hooked Pennell tackle. Hook sizes vary from 8 to 4/0 according to the size of bait and species of fish.

52 Fresh herring filleted and cut into strips. Both herrings and mackerel are prepared this way. Neat cutting makes more attractive baits and is more economical.

Herrings and mackerel

A popular bait, second only to worms, fish baits are perfect for most of the bigger predators and may be cut into small pieces in order to attract the smaller species.

The only fish baits worth using are those you have caught yourself, or that you are certain came fresh from the commercial boats. If you cannot be sure of catching your own mackerel, go directly to the quayside for supplies. It is possible to catch herrings on rod and line,

53 A complete mackerel fillet mounted on conger tackle. The hook point is well proud of the bait for better penetration, and the fillet is secured to the trace with a short length of cotton.

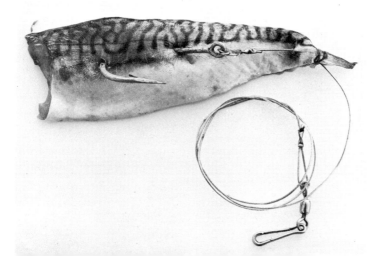

54 Herring strip mounted on the hook. It is not necessary to cram the bait on to the hook shank; just a couple of nicks under the skin hold the bait firmly yet allow it to move in the water currents.

but never specifically for baiting purposes. Again, buy them from the longshore netsmen.

CARE

Keep them cool and moist, never allowing direct sunlight to dry them out, and in a cooler box all the time when out fishing. If cooler boxes are not available, freshly caught mackerel will last a little longer immersed in a bucket of cold seawater.

LONG-TERM STORAGE

Fish may be individually wrapped in plastic film and deepfrozen.

PRESENTATION

Mackerel straight from the sea can be used as livebaits for big tope and bass. If whole fish are too big, the fishes are filleted or cut into chunks. Mackerel and herring heads are good baits too. The flesh withstands reasonably hard casting when thawed, but long-range work is easier with packaged or hard-frozen fish. The fillets and chunks are secured by nicking the hookpoint through the flesh and into the skin. Whole fish are mounted by threading the trace right the way through, then securing it with a few strands of cotton. The rule is to leave the hookpoint proud of the bait; otherwise it will bury itself into the bait, not into the fish that picks it up.

Squid

A good but erratic bait that becomes popular in cycles, then fades from the scene for a while, squid is often used in combination with other

baits.

55 Squid is an excellent bait for most species, and seems to attract the bigger specimens. Small squids are used whole; the bigger ones are cut into strips. The head is good for ground fishing and for use as a sink-and-draw lure.

It is imported deepfrozen from California, and bought in blocks from bait dealers and fishmongers.

CARE

Keep it cool in an insulated box: nothing in the world smells worse than rotten squid; the juices seep into everything.

LONG-TERM STORAGE

Deepfrozen blocks may be sawn, without thawing, into more manageable chunks.

PRESENTATION

Squid is very tough, and may be used whole or cut into strips. It is almost impossible to cast from the hook and withstands shrimp and crab attack. For some reason squid tends to catch the big fish. If you are willing to wait for just one big fish, this is the bait. The head can be used as a moving lure jerked along the seabed.

Crabs

One of the finest baits of all, crabs were once considered so superior that they were banned from fishing matches. They are really excellent for most species of fish. Any species of crab is good. Most are seldom

91

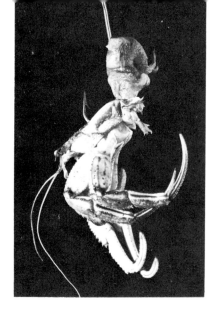

56 A hermit crab removed from its shell and mounted on the hook ready for casting. All species of crabs can be mounted in the same manner by threading them up the hook shank then securing with a few turns of cotton.

used, because they live in deep water and cannot be collected except by net. The common shore crab is picked up from tidepools and under rocks and weeds along the foreshore. Hermit crabs live in deeper water and may be caught in a dropnet baited with pieces of fish. Sometimes edible crabs are found under stones. They are good baits, but it must be remembered that specimens measuring less than 4 in (10 cm) across the carapace are immature and protected. All crabs undergo moulting when the old shell is outgrown. After the shell comes off, the new one is soft for a few days, during which the crab is vulnerable. Soft crabs and peelers—the stage where the old shell is ready to shuck—are better baits than hardbacked crabs. Hermit crabs do not shed the suit of armour because most of their body is naturally soft, and protected by the whelk shell in which they normally lodge.

SUPPLY

Crabs are gathered from under stones and weeds; they live almost anywhere, though are prolific on rough ground. Tackle shops may sell them, but supplies are erratic and very expensive. The best way to get lots of crabs is to hitch a ride on an inshore trawler and sort through the freshly hauled nets.

CARE

Keep them under seaweed in a damp box with a splash of saltwater in the bottom. Never keep crabs in plastic bags. Soft and peeler crabs must be kept apart, or the peelers kill their neighbours.

LONG-TERM STORAGE

92 Crabs may be deep frozen in a freezing fluid that reduces tissue damage.

57 *Peeling shore crabs in a wooden bait box. Kept damp and covered, the creatures will live for a week or more.*

Dissolve ⅛ oz (3.5 g) of common salt in every 4 fl oz (100 ml) of water, then stir in a generous half teaspoonful (3 ml) of glycerol. Place the crabs in a plastic bag, cover them with the fluid, then freeze.

PRESENTATION

Peelers are shelled and used whole or cut into pieces. The legs and claws are good baits for small fish. Soft crabs are treated in the same way, but of course there is no need to remove the shell. To mount a whole crab, pass the hook once through the centre of the body, then tie one set of legs to the hook shank with a strip of elastic band or a few turns of cotton. The hook size obviously conforms to the species of fish and to the overall size of the bait.

SECONDARY BAITS: SHELLFISH

Limpets

Some shorelines are peppered with native limpets that graze over rocks. They are very tough on the hook and juicy enough to attract fishes. Most limpets are used in deep water to lure wrasse and other seabed feeders. They may be prised off rocks and stored in a can of seawater, but are usually so prolific that collection is a waste of time: you just chip one off the rock each time you bait the hook.

The slipper limpet was introduced into Britain about 60 years ago, since when it has spread around the coast to colonise vast areas.

93

58 Hermit crabs. The crab lives in a discarded shell—usually a whelk shell—and can be caught in a small trawl or by baited dropnet. It is a superb bait for most species of fishes.

Bunches of limpets resembling stacks of coins are good baits locally, but not always so effective farther away. They may be kept for years salted or frozen.

Razorfish

Razorfish are thin-shelled bivalves that live on the lowest limits of spring tides. They are fast-burying, vibration-sensitive creatures which demand a certain knack for successful capture. You can spear them, dig them up or tickle them to the surface by pouring salt down the key-shaped hole. Very good baits for a range of fishes, and a firm, meaty offering that stands up to hard casting quite well, they keep in the freezer for months.

Mussels

Littoral beds stretch for miles in some parts of the country where there are low rocks washed by the incoming tide. On the North Coast of England and in Scotland mussels are a deadly bait for the native cod, haddock and flatfishes. They may be mounted fresh or after toughening in steam. Mussel beds are always associated with plaice.

Other shellfish

Clams, whelks, scallops and most other species are good baits. Scallops and clams are really excellent for many species but are fairly difficult to obtain. The collection of scallops and whelks involves dredging with a small beam trawl or, in the latter case, trapping with a baited dropnet. The whelk is not so good from the shore as it is out to sea. Many commercial longliners use whelk baits almost exclusively for cod, dogfish and whiting. Inshore results may not be as good.

Shellfish are sometimes better used as an expander to make the worm and fish baits go further. Clam siphons and the tough foot of whelks make a good buffer that helps keep softer baits attached to the hook for long-distance casting. The flesh also acts as a visual attractor.

SHRIMPS, PRAWNS, SMALL FISHES AND SANDEELS

If you drop a dead worm or small piece of fish into shallow water and stand so that your shadow does not fall across it, the bait seems to come alive after a couple of minutes. Close examination reveals a mass of almost transparent shrimps or prawns. These creatures are so prolific in some inshore waters that they become a major food of a variety of fishes. Running a handnet through shallows amongst weeds and rocks soon fills a can of seawater with hundreds of superb baits which may be legered for flatfishes, floated for bass, ground up into tiny mullet baits or be mashed into groundbait. Those that remain after fishing can be boiled for tea.

Blennies, butterfish and elvers lurk under rocks and in pools. They are often found when you are looking for crabs. Any small, lively creature may be considered a potential bait and should be kept safely in a can of water. Small fishes may be used live or dead, by leger, float and spinning techniques. Any that remain after fishing will store well in the freezer.

Sandeels are perhaps the most underestimated bait in Britain. Few predatory fishes refuse them; from tope down to flounders, they snap them up in preference to almost any other bait. Unfortunately sandeels, like many unusual baits, are localised in distribution and difficult to collect. At low tide in estuary channels you can rake them out of the sand. Digging is possible but quite a pantomime, as eels skitter away and sand flies everywhere. Easiest of all is running a net across the channel, the method adopted by professional bait collectors. Huge numbers are netted very quickly, graded into various sizes and frozen to ensure absolute freshness.

Because the size range is great, many anglers select the whole sandeel that suits their fishing; but chunks cut from the bigger eels are just as effective. Frozen eels are ideal for legering, floatfishing and spinning, but live ones are possibly deadliest of all. Live eels are hooked once through the jaw or into the skin on the back. Dead, they are mounted in the same way as fish baits.

8 Floatfishing

Plankton and other tiny marine creatures migrate between surface and deep water in circadian and seasonal rhythms determined by temperature, light intensity and the nutrient levels of the saltwater. Small fry and the lesser predators—sandeels, garfish and mackerel—follow them, and they in turn are intercepted by the big predatory fishes. The bigger species may hunt at varying depths but are more likely to patrol at preferred levels. Over a reef and close to the sheer faces of underwater cliffs, rays, conger eels and wrasse lurk on or near the seabed, pollack lie above them, and mackerel, garfish, mullet and sandeels swim midwater to just below the surface. At certain times, particularly dawn and sunset, a general migration occurs: mackerel herd the fry and sandeels to the surface, and are themselves harried by pollack and even tope. In bad weather and during the winter, the fishes may stay deeper or move away altogether.

Fishing methods that anchor baits on the seabed are therefore of limited use in very deep water. Float tackle is better because it allows bait presentation at carefully controlled depths; additionally, it is one of the few techniques that help discrimination between species. You can hook pollack instead of wrasse by raising the baits out of the deepest gulleys to the rockfaces above. Wrasse seem reluctant to swim upwards for baits even 3 ft (0.9 m) over their heads and seldom bother to chase them into pollack territory. Some species have no set depth and may be on the surface one minute, on the bottom the next. Mackerel sometimes hunt along the bottom, though it is more common to find them midwater or near the surface.

Floatfished baits are easily located because many predators isolate their prey against the light, then attack from below. A drifting bait exudes its own scent trail, and its effect is further enhanced by visual attraction and movement, either natural or wave-induced. Another important advantage of the rig is to reduce tackle losses over rough ground. Rough ground and deep water often go together: the inshore seabed of many prolific rockfishing places is crammed with obstructions. To cast leger tackle is to lose sinker and trace at least; pulling for a break takes yards of the reel line. Most floatfishing methods present baits upwards of 1 ft (30 cm) from the bottom, which prevent many losses, but even if the baits must be fished right on the seabed modified float tackle saves time and money. You do lose tackle, but nowhere near so much as with conventional legering.

On some shores it is impossible or unnecessary to fish with floats.

59 *Floatfishing tackle is at its best from rocks and piers where short casting puts the baits into deep water. In many respects a pier is similar to rocks and reefs: the pilings form a habitat in which species stratification occurs. Floated baits present the baits at the right depth and away from seabed snags.*

Cod and whiting beaches, shallow estuaries and surfstrands are fishing grounds where floats have little to commend their use. Water less than 20 ft (6 m) deep is better covered by ground fishing or spinning unless the fish are feeding just under the surface. It is most unlikely that stratification of species will occur in shallow water, so the rig cannot be used to hunt one particular species which in deeper water patrols at a certain depth. But outside the obvious limitations of shorelines, shallows and very fast tides, the float rig is extremely versatile and could be used more often than it is. **97**

TACKLE FOR FLOATFISHING

The lightest of sea tackle is far too heavy for most mullet fishing. Freshwater rods and light lines are essential to help allay fear. The terminal tackle must be assembled with great attention to detail and take into account their feeding habits. Harbour mullet, accustomed to the rotting carcases of fish thrown over the side of commercial fishing boats, search for their food on the seabed and very light legers are useful. But the bulk of mullet fishing is by float: tiny quills and dust shot present the baits as delicately as possible, and sometimes the bait should be cast with no additional weights at all. The fish then take the offering as it falls slowly. At the other extreme, mullet on the surface might refuse any bait not suspended at the top of the water by surface tension.

Ultra-light float tackle can seldom be used in the open sea because the swells wash it away even on the calmest day. Sinker weights less than $\frac{1}{2}$ oz (15 g) are unlikely to drag the baits deep enough anyway. Except for open-coast mullet, which are often even more neurotic than those in harbours, it is more realistic to upgrade the tackle to a spinning rod, 10–15 lb (4.5–6.8 kg) line and matching fixed-spool reel. Tackle of this class is ideal for average-weight wrasse and pollack, mackerel and bass. In many respects it is best of all for really good fun with normal-sized fishes.

Increasing rod and line strength gives you more muscle, and unless taken to extremes there is no reason why greater tackle weight should normally deter fish from biting. Lines from 15–20 lb (6.8–9.1 kg) coupled to matched rods and reels are a more sensible choice if you

60 A lightweight fixed-spool reel loaded with 6–15 lb (2·7–6·8 kg) line is the best reel for floatfishing because it allows easier casting with the light sinkers and bulky floats.

suspect that your fishing place holds some of the bigger specimens. Whatever the average size of the fish, strong tackle is necessary to combat wind and swells. A moderate swell churning against the rocks will not deter the fish from feeding, but does prevent the sinker going down far enough. On light line, even 1 oz (30 g) of lead washes around in the foam with the baits sunk just under the surface. You need lots of weight to get the baits deep enough; sometimes even 6 oz (170 g) is needed to fish deep-water marks in a gale.

Super-heavy float tackle has a place in the specimen hunter's armoury. The big pelagic predators, tope and sharks, prefer a floated bait to one anchored on the bottom: 4–6 oz (115–170 g) tackle rigged with a balloon float may be cast well out into the tidestream. The tiderace on the end of exposed headlands is a favourite haunt of tope, sharks, big pollack, rays and congers. Baits floated downtide, either in midwater or tripping the bottom, are deadly.

FIXING TACKLE DEPTH

When baits are fished less than 10 ft (3 m) from the surface, the float may be attached firmly to the reel line. At greater depth, it is impossible to cast a fixed float, and the tackle must be altered so that the float slides freely on the line, stopped at depth by a stop knot. The stop knot needs to pass through the rod rings for casting, so it must be as neat as possible. A short piece of elastic band clove-hitched to the nylon is cheap and very effective. Although the float slides towards the trace for casting, it should not come so close that it tangles in the trace or baits. Tangling is always a problem in floatfishing, and no matter how smooth the cast, the terminal rig whirls around in midair. One way to be reasonably sure that the float keeps its distance is to tie a second stop knot below the float so that it slides no closer than 3 ft (0.9 m) to the trace. Tangles are never eliminated, though, and therefore smooth, gentle casts are to be preferred.

Fishing depth depends upon the nature of the seabed and the habits of the species. Heavy ground with pinnacles of rock and tangles of kelp ensnares tackle that comes too near. The maximum depth for safe fishing is that which avoids all but the tallest obstructions. But although seabed topography influences tackle depth, baits must be set so that the fish can find them; if that means losing tackle, too bad. Searching for the right depth is a hit-and-miss affair unless a system is adopted. If you know that your quarry lives near the bottom, set the baits very deep, then work upwards 1 ft (30 cm) at a time until bites appear. Conversely, mackerel and bass swimming high in the water are better located by working the tackle downwards.

The tendency in floatfishing is to fish far too shallow. It is surprising how long it takes for a sinker to hit bottom. In 20 fathoms (37 m), 1 oz (30 g) of lead could take over half a minute to drag the baits right down. In really rough water, 4 or even 6 oz (115 or 170 g) take just as long. Because most anglers do not appreciate how slowly tackle sinks, they fish too near the surface. Sometimes that is not seriously wrong, but

61 Inshore weeds and rocks that snag the line can be avoided by float tackle used either conventionally or by the suspended line modification.

with species like wrasse shallow baits are a waste of time. If you should ever fish a known wrasse mark without getting bites, look to the fishing depth. By going too deep you risk tackle losses, but it is better to lose a few traces than to catch nothing.

Some fishes are tempted by a bait drifting slowly downwards from the surface. Use minimum sinker weight and allow the tackle to take all the time in the world—perhaps 5 minutes to sink 10 fathoms (18 m). The method is particularly effective when the fish are reluctant to feed, or if they are so well scattered that conventional techniques fail to pinpoint them.

TACKLE MOVEMENT AND WATER SEARCHING

The rise and fall of breakers washes baits around undersea gulleys and into the crannies where fish lurk. A good swell lifts the tackle several feet, then lets it flutter down in the backwash, all of which increases the attraction. The darting movement alone might trigger an attack. The lateral sweep of waves and currents expands the search area, but unless you want the tackle to remain stationary it is probably better to allow it to roam, even though there is a greater risk of snagging on rocks. Normal tides and breezes provide a steady drift, but gales and spring tides speed the float so that the baits rush through the water. The faster the drift, the more the tackle rises, which is obviously bad practice. Flowing water is almost impossible to master except by waiting for the slack-water periods when the currents ceases or slows. Wind sails the float and line leewards at a terrific rate, but anything less than a gale can be dealt with by reducing float size and sinking the rod tip so that the wind cannot bow it. The technique is so effective that the tackle might stop altogether, but you need only raise the rod to sail it away once more.

Tide flow can be an ally. On headlands and piers the current often flows directly away from you. It is easy to lob out the tackle and drift it hundreds of yards. Vast areas are covered, which is of great advantage in tope and ray fishing when the fish are well scattered. Light tackle is fished at full tide speed; if a slower drift is necessary, use heavier sinkers to prevent bait rising too far from the bottom. A particularly good method of attracting garfish and other surface feeders is light

62 Assorted floats for seafishing. Commercially made floats of wood, cork and plastic are excellent, but on really rough ground where tackle losses are high it makes more sense to use simple home-made floats like the plastic canister shown here.

tackle drifted for a few yards, braked so that the baits swing to the top, then released again. Fishes often hit the baits as they rise and flutter down.

HITTING THE BITES

As in all other branches of shorefishing, there are no stereotyped bite patterns. The float might skitter along the surface, sink in a whirlpool of its own making, or just flicker from side to side. Sometimes you strike because the float looks wrong or because its rhythm changes. As in legering, there is the same tendency to overreact and to snatch the baits away. In my experience, unless the bite is so firm that the line tightens by itself, it pays to wait. Count slowly to five before reeling. Of course, this is never completely reliable: delay might give the fish time to dive for the weeds. But on average, later is best. Bait size affects the bite speed and consequently the strike delay. Small fragments of bait are gulped down faster than a whole side of mackerel would be. Rays and flatfishes need more time than do the fast predators.

Because it is normally short-range work, striking is sometimes effective in floatfishing. You can hit the rod hard enough to drive in the hook; and the jerk brings the fish's head up for a moment so that you can hustle him away from the rocks and weeds. Disorientated in this way, a pollack forgets to dive long enough for you to get him into open water. This element of surprise tips the balance in your favour over very rough ground and allows the use of lighter tackle than might otherwise be necessary. Once the fish is hooked, playing and landing are the same as in any other branch of fishing.

SUSPENDED-LINE FISHING

A good way of surveying the seabed is to cast out a plain sinker, let it sink, then slowly reel in. With experience you can hazard a guess at the nature of the bottom: sand and mud feel smooth, small rocks, shingle and scattered weeds grate and momentarily snag the line. Many deep-water marks investigated this way reveal an absolutely clean seabed from about 30 yds (or 30 m) to maximum casting range. Unless they are truly pelagic, the species of fishes in the area seem to enjoy life near the bottom. Rays, flatfishes and bass like the open ground, and even congers and wrasse move there from their usual haunts among the gulleys. Night-time is favourite: sandy patches are stiff with feeding fishes from sunset onwards. The best fishing technique is obviously to place a stationary bait right on the seabed—in other words, legering.

Legering is often impossible because every time you try to reel in the line snags. If you hook a fish it comes so far, then stops. In both cases the cause is the sunken line catching on inshore rocks and weeds. Offshore, the seabed is clean; your survey proved it. There may have been obstructions closer in, but surely not this many? What you failed to consider is that line sinks in time. As you cast and retrieved the plain sinker, the line never had time to fall because it was constantly moving.

But as soon as the baits were cast and the rod propped in its rest, the line sank straight into the inshore snags. When you came to reel in, the line was firmly caught, and the obstruction acted like a pulley that guided the tackle straight into the rocks. Once there it stuck fast.

Conventional float tackle prevents tackle losses but seldom allows firm bait anchorage—an important consideration for rays and congers. Any wind or tide sweeps the baits off the clear patches. You must get the baits hard down on the bottom, and only the leger will do it. In these circumstances suspended-line tackle might be the answer. This is either a paternoster or a running leger with the reel line buoyed by a float (fig 22). For convenience and cheapness partially inflated balloons are ideal. The terminal rig is assembled normally except that a split ring is clipped on to the reel line and stopped from sliding down to the trace by a stop knot. Then the balloon is attached to the ring by a short link of nylon.

Cast the tackle as normal, anchor the sinker, then wind in the slack line. The balloon will hold it up, well away from the inshore snags. The essential difference between suspended tackle and conventional float tackle is the omission of the upper stop knot. The balloon is completely free to slide on the line and does not take the weight of the terminal rig. It tends to lag behind during the cast, settling some 50 yds (45 m) out. This is the ideal position for it to hold up the line and there should be no problem with inshore line sinking too deep. If it does, the reel line is too slack.

The float is not used as a bite indicator, though sometimes it does signal the presence of a fish by skittering. It has a further advantage though: retrieved line comes back at such an angle that the tackle lifts

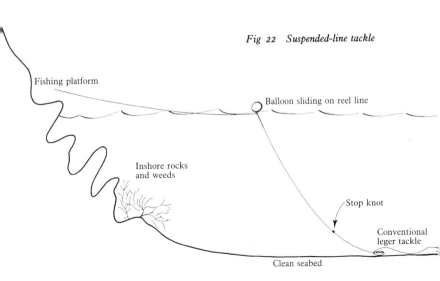

Fig 22 Suspended-line tackle

Fishing platform

Balloon sliding on reel line

Inshore rocks
and weeds

Stop knot

Conventional
leger tackle

Clean seabed

63 *Really huge fishes like this bass of over 13 lb (5.9 kg) prefer wild water and rough seabeds. Floated tackle helps you put the bait in the right place, and get the hooked fish ashore.*

from the seabed. The faster the retrieve the better, so it is beneficial to use either a fast multiplier or even a fixed-spool. Fixed-spool reels are usually so highly geared as to be useless, but here they excel provided that the tackle is reasonably light.

The rig is also good for legering on rough ground. Species like congers and some rays demand baits on the seabed. On many occasions they feed very slowly and therefore tend to ignore floating baits that drift past. Rays and congers take up residence in certain spots, which they are reluctant to leave. They are ambush feeders who have all the time in the world to sit there and watch life roll by. If a bait trundles past in the tide they will ignore it unless it bumps into their noses. On the other hand, they will venture a little way for a bait that has been lying on the seabed long enough to attract attention. To hold that bait on the bottom you need leger tackle. Suspending the line helps prevent losses because the angle of the line lifts the tackle away from the seabed on retrieve.

Tackle losses are inevitable, so it makes sense to use a disposable rig. Strip the terminal tackle down to the bare bones: no swivels or booms, no expensive moulded lead sinkers. Old nuts and bolts, stones, chunks of scrap iron and discarded sparking plugs are the sinkers to use. Old sparking plugs are particularly useful because they weigh a convenient 2½–3 oz (70–85 g). All disposable weights can be attached by lighter line which, in theory, should break before the main line. In practice the hook is far more likely to snag than is the sinker. It is silly to attach the hook by lighter trace material, though—just accept losses as being part of the game.

9 *Fishing with artificial lures*

It is very much easier to catch predatory fishes on legered or floated, dead, natural baits. Spinners and plug lures are often less successful in terms of numbers of fishes hooked. The subjective difference between natural and artificial baits is that only lures trigger the chase-and-kill instinct. A pollack that picks up a chunk of legered mackerel is never the same fierce hunter that smashes into a spinner. For that reason alone, artificial-lure fishing will always reign supreme in saltwater angling as it does in salmon and trout fishing. Gamefish the world over hit artificial lures; if they did not, they would not be gamefish.

British coastal waters are woefully lacking in game species. The fishes that hit lures are generally small and, without exception, outclassed by the bonefish, tarpon and striped bass which anglers in other countries enjoy. To this must be added the general unsuitability for lure fishing of most inshore waters. Except where the North Atlantic Drift pulses clear oceanic water along the shoreline, inshore seas are often clouded with silt. Water clarity is not necessarily a prerequisite for successful lure fishing, but it certainly helps. The combination of all these factors makes spinning a minor technique in British seafishing. It need not be: there are many times when it is as good if not better than floatfishing and legering. And it is always much more exciting.

A knowledge of natural history lays the foundation to successful lure fishing. If your quarry is mackerel, for instance, you need to realise that the fishes are likely to fall for a lure simulating the sandeels, fry and smaller mackerel that make up their diet. According to season and time of day, you would hunt them in the surface layers or closer to the seabed. On the other hand, coalfish lying in ambush alongside weeds and rocks demands a different lure presentation.

The guidance systems that enable the killers to home in on their victims are poorly understood. It is thought that primary detection is by the lateral line, which enables the fish to intercept vibrations from its prey and also to use its own vibrations as a kind of sonar. The final stage comes when the victim is very close: once the range is short, eyesight takes over and allows accurate positioning for the assault.

LURE DESIGN

The physiology of the fish's eye and its nervous system suggests that the predatory fishes have better eyesight than the rest, but even so the eyes react more to movement and contrast. Acuity of vision, and even colour

64 *Many predatory fish lurk near underwater obstructions to pounce on smaller fishes that drift past. A lure pulled through the water triggers the same attack reaction.*

perception, might be secondary. Certainly, there is not the highly detailed picture that mammalian eyes produce. Precise imitation is therefore unnecessary in lure design; if the outline is reasonably accurate and the coloration of good contrast to the surroundings, the lure will deceive.

All artificial lures, be they spinners, plugs, jigs or squids, are essentially vibration generators. Visual attraction is less effective as the range increases and may be regarded as the final inducement: on most occasions the fish has decided to attack before he sees the lure. Vibration stems from wobbling, spinning, jerking and turbulence, and may be induced by vanes on the lure that cause it to roll and twist, by the rod and reel action, or by propeller blades on the spinner body. Whatever the mechanism, the lure emits vibrations of various frequencies. The initial effect on the fish is to draw its attention. It might be thought that because the sea is constantly moving and therefore very noisy, the lure's pulses are too weak to notice. That is not so: the beat of waves and the squeaks and clicking sounds made by other fish are part of the normal underwater background. In the same way that people living beside busy motorways cease to notice the constant traffic roar, so a fish will screen out the background, and any strange noise is easily recognised.

Strong vibratory patterns are essential in a lure, and the design should allow them to be generated at the correct speed. Slow lures must pulse strongly at low speeds, and this is better achieved by fitting the lure with spinning vanes or propellers. Fast lures normally create sufficient turbulence without the need for vanes, but anything that boosts the pulsation is to the good. On the other hand, too much drag from blades and propellers makes the lure difficult to fish fast.

Outline and coloration are secondary attractors but important none the less. The question of size is really commonsense: use a lure similar in size to the bait fish you are seeking to imitate. Coloration is a vexed question. All you can say is that some fishes, sometimes, prefer certain colours. Contrast is obviously important in separating the lure from its background. Dark colours appear in sharp silhouette against a backdrop of open water; the same ones would be less prominent against a backing

65 Light tackle, a spinner and deep water: a combination that leads to superb sport with pollack, bass and mackerel.

of weeds and rocks, where a golden, silver or light tone might work better. In my experience gold works well, as do white and silver-blue. The darker shades of red or even black work better at certain times, particularly at sunset and after dark. The selection of colours certainly depends on a few factors that we do not recognise, let alone understand. Red light is quickly absorbed by the surface layers of water, and deep down red appears black. Yet sometimes fish ignore a black lure and slam into a red one, which, colour excepted, is absolutely identical to the first. Experiment and experience are the keys to lure selection; and whatever the rules might be, some fishes, somewhere, will break them.

Lures can be made from plastics, feathers and metals. All work well if the design is correct, but some types are better for use in the sea because their weight gives longer casting range. Casting far enough is always a problem with lures, and a certain amount of inherent weight is necessary to sink the device through swells. Good lures are fairly heavy—$\frac{1}{2}$–2 oz (15–55 g) normally—and of metal. If possible, all the weight should be incorporated in the lure itself, not attached to the trace. Extra sinkers detract from the lure's action and promote tangling during the cast. The only lure always used with a sinker is the string of feathers, and this is one case where nothing is lost by adding weight. Never use plugs with extra sinkers, though; the action is totally destroyed by even the tiniest addition to the trace.

There are thousands of different designs. Selection can only be by trial and error, though it is possible to begin with a cross-section of the commoner types: small propeller spinners; small and medium and large bar spoons and German Sprats; small and medium Redgill sandeels (also to be used with an up-trace sinker in deep water), or plastic sandeels; and all the various strings of feathers suitable for use from the shoreline. This range will allow you to fish for anything from garfish to pollack. With experience, most anglers seem to settle on two or three favourites. Given the choice of two types only, I would have a 2 in (5 cm) lure such as the Abu Toby, and some Redgills.

66 *The treble hook fitted to a lure will suffer from severe corrosion if not looked after. This hook is useless and would snap on the first fish that hit the lure.*

Lure maintenance is vital. Because they are soon lost, lures are regarded as disposable and not worth the bother of looking after in the same way that reels and rods are. They should be washed in freshwater after every trip to the sea. Saltwater attacks metals, and the metal themselves destroy each other by galvanic action. Split rings, swivels and hooks are most at risk; it is not uncommon to have one of these links snap soon after a big fish is hooked. Lubrication seems a bad idea, though: if a lure is tainted with oil or grease you sometimes find that no bites occur until the tackle has been in the water long enough to wash out the lubricants.

TACKLE FOR SPINNING

Feathering and long-range, deep-water spinning might require normal beachcasting rods. Specialised lure rods about 9 ft (2.7 m) long and casting up to 2 oz (55 g) are ideal for most work though, and are the preferred tackle for routine inshore work. The reel is normally one of the smaller fixed-spools, because casting light lures is easier on a stationary-spooled reel. Multipliers work better with at least 1 oz (30 g) of weight to get the spool turning fast enough. But if the multiplier will cast far enough it is better for playing a fish. Lines obviously need to match the rest of the tackle, and leaders are not compulsory. It is, however, good practice to include a short 15–20 lb (6.8–9.1 kg) leader when fishing really rough ground, so that the trace is not too soon abraded by the rocks. Sometimes, too, the leader makes a good towrope for pulling fish ashore if you cannot get close enough with a gaff or net.

SEARCHING THE WATER
Deep water

The fishes in deep water will normally feed at a set depth, and ignore baits that are too deep or over their heads. If they are shoaling on the surface, there is no doubt where to cast. Mackerel tearing into shoals of sandeels and brit just under the surface snatch lures worked fast right under their noses. More often though, the fish are deeper and there is no broken water or swirls to indicate their presence. Then the lure must be worked in a pattern that covers all the water from surface to seabed. Haphazard casting and retrieve are no substitutes for a proper search. A further complication of many deep-water marks—rocks and cliffs, for instance—is limited access. When he is fishing, the angler cannot move along the shoreline and might have to cover all the water from one station. A simple method of covering a great deal of sea in both depth and area is the radial pattern (fig 23).

The casting area is covered by throwing the lure either to the right or left along the shoreline, then placing subsequent casts so that they radiate like wheel spokes from the central hub. The water is searched foot by foot in a complete semicircle, and also by casting progressive distances. Sometimes it takes thirty casts to cover all the water in a 50 yds (45 m) radius. This might seem too fussy, but it is amazing how

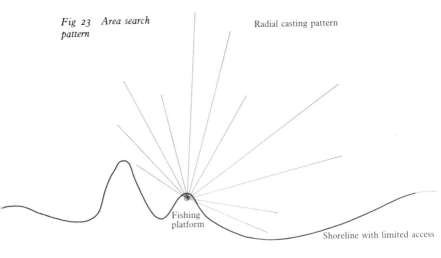

Fig 23 *Area search pattern*

Radial casting pattern

Fishing platform

Shoreline with limited access

many times you get fish from places where just a dozen random casts yield nothing.

The depth search (fig 24) is even more important. As in floatfishing, the tendency is to fish too high in the water, a problem aggravated by the almost unbelievable time it takes for a lure to sink deeply. A 1 oz (30 g) lure on light line takes anything up to a minute to sink to the seabed. An average of 5 seconds per fathom (nearly 3 per metre) is not excessive, and may need greatly increasing in swells. The only way to be sure that the lure has reached full depth is waiting until the line slackens right off. To establish a depth scale, count slowly from the moment the lure splashes down until the reel line slackens. Suppose it took 30 seconds. Assuming that the lure sinks at a regular pace—in fact

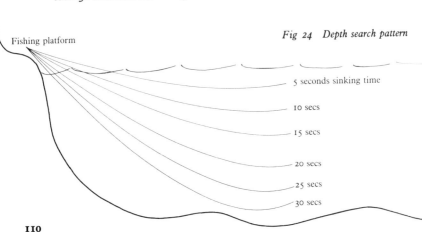

Fishing platform

Fig 24 *Depth search pattern*

5 seconds sinking time

10 secs

15 secs

20 secs

25 secs

30 secs

it slows towards the end but that makes little difference as a rule—you can fish midwater by counting to 15 seconds before reeling. To locate fish by combing the water from top to bottom, vary the delay by increments: begin to wind at 5, 10, 15, 20 seconds and so on. If the depth search is combined with the radial pattern, you are sure of fishing every inch of water within casting range.

It should become routine to allow line to peel off the spool as the lure sinks. Only then can you be reasonably sure of maintaining full casting

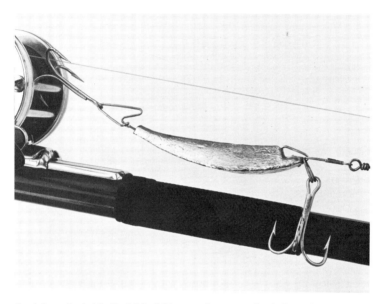

67 A heavy lead pirk. Useful for fishing very deep water close inshore where there are big cod, pollack and coalfish.

distance. A further problem in lure work is keeping at a set depth, because lures tend to rise. Work the tackle as slowly as conditions and lure design permit, but if it must run fast, stop occasionally to let it fall back to the proper level. Rising on retrieve can be an advantage if you are unsure of the depth at which the fish are patrolling. Also, it might pay to ignore the rule about releasing line as the lure sinks after casting. Held tight, the tackle falls in an arc that brings it quickly inshore. As the lure fluttered down towards the rockfaces, a fish might attack. It is a very good way to fish the rocks and weeds right under your feet in very deep water. And it is amazing how many of the really big specimens are that close inshore.

Open beaches

Open beaches and shallow water may be fished without the depth search, because unless the water is over 20 ft (6 m) deep it will not work anyway. Neither is the radial pattern necessary if you are free to walk along the shore. In really fast water you cannot use the radial casting method because all the casts that go upstream are washed down again before the lure comes under the line's control. Cast varying ranges, retrieve slowly, at high speed, smoothly, in jerks; anything to break the monotony. Generally it is better to keep the lure above the seabed, but there are occasions when a pirk or squid jerked along on the bottom hooks more fish. This often happens with surfstrand bass: a lure kicking up clouds of sand is deadly. I think bass confuse the disturbance with the characteristic sandstorm thrown up by frightened flatfishes, sandeels and crustaceans. The explanation might also extend

68 Metal spinning lures and spoons used to lure most predatory seafishes.

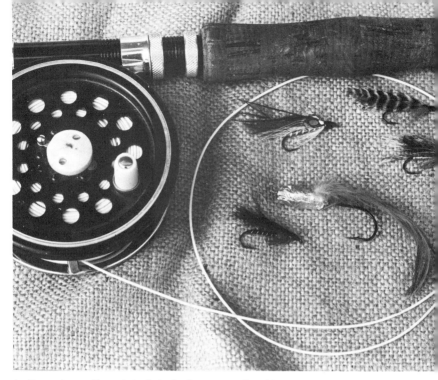

69 *Reservoir trout flies and simple feather lures cast on fly tackle give excellent sport with shoaling bass, mackerel and garfish. Flyfishing is one aspect of British shorefishing severely neglected, and for no good reason.*

to the reason why a moving leger often takes more fish from surfstrands.

BAITED LURES

Sometimes a lure fished right under the fish's nose is ignored. This is perfectly-understandable, because most predators feed in cycles, and when they are not out for blood may completely switch off. Sandeels may be seen to swim alongside shoals of pollack which 10 minutes earlier were slashing at them. A kind of truce has followed and both sides mix freely—until next time. An artificial lure, being in the fish's eye just another marine creature, is disregarded too. Occasionally you can induce the predator to snap at the lure by drawing it so close and so often that the fish seems to lose its temper.

An even better strategy is adding baits to the lure so as to boost attraction by scent and taste. The technique is of value when the fishes are feeding, but only halfheartedly. They might peck at the lure rather than slam into it in the usual manner. Almost any natural bait may be added provided that the lure's action is not too swamped by the load. Slivers of fish (the belly of mackerel is excellent), squid, ragworms and even the humble lugworm are all good attractors. The treble hook normally supplied with the lure is not ideal for baits and may be exchanged for a long-shanked single. In fact there are several advantages to singles anyway: they are less likely to snag and easier to drive home because all the strike force is concentrated on one point, not spread over two or three.

FEATHERING

A string of six or seven feathers imitates a shoal of bait fish. If predators are feeding at high speed, lowering a string in their vicinity sometimes results in a full house: a fish on every hook. The value of catching them like this is more or less restricted to bait collection; after the first few casts there is no sport in the fishing. On the other hand, feathers fished sink-and-draw are very good for sorting out some of the seabed species. The method is further enhanced by baiting the lures. Single feathers are a different matter. They are very sporting, and just as effective as the most expensive lure. A couple of seagull feathers whipped to a hook and weighted down by a strip of lead make a beautiful lure, and one so cheap that you can afford to lose it among the rocks and weeds in really foul ground. And if there are any really big fish around, they will be in the worst of the undersea jungle.

70 A floating plug bait. Another lure seldom used in British waters yet, like the fly tackle, of enormous potential.

10 *Looking after the catch*

Fish deteriorates very quickly. After a few hours in the sun and wind the skin withers into leather, flies crawl all over it and the flesh begins to rot as internal autolysis speeds up. Unhooking a newly caught fish and throwing it high up the beach to fend for itself while you continue to fish is no way to carry on. From the moment it comes splashing out of the sea, a fish needs care.

First comes the moral obligation: if you intend to keep the fish, kill it. Hit it on the head with a rock or sever the spinal cord with a knife. Fishing is a bloodsport, it is cruel, and there are many organisations that want to ban it. As sportsmen we owe it to our quarry and to ourselves to minimise cruelty and pain. Killing fish is a moral question, and like any other issue of its kind must be the decision of the man taking part. If you kill fish, as I do, that is your privilege and nobody has any right to question it. But ethically, and for the good of angling, it must be done immediately and well.

Gutting is the next step. The sooner the internal organs are removed the less chance there is of autolysis and unnecessary putrefaction. Doing the job on the beach has the added advantages of getting rid of the waste before taking the fish home, and also washing away the blood and excess slime in saltwater, which is much better than fresh water. The technique is so simple that detailed descriptions are unwarranted. Insert a sharp knife into the vent and cut the skin along to the ventral fins. Open the gut cavity and shake out the contents. Sever the intestinal tract top and bottom with a few strokes of the knife, scrape out the swim-bladder and superficial skin and veins, then wash out the blood.

The offal is no use except perhaps for the roe and liver, but even they are too small for a meal unless you catch many fish or some very big ones. All the waste can be thrown into the sea where the gulls and crabs make short work of it. It is always worth opening the stomach. The contents are an excellent guide to the fish's diet and also to the predominant foodstuff in the area. Many a fish has been caught on a dead crab, fish or shellfish taken from another's stomach.

Rays are more difficult to clean because of their shape and extreme sliminess. The first cut should be around the borders of the gut cavity, which is then exposed by pulling back the flap of loose skin. Pull out all the organs, then cut through the gills and down the cavity margins to let the blood run out (see Plate 71). Blood vessels in the wings will rupture after death and taint the flesh unless this step is taken as soon as possible.

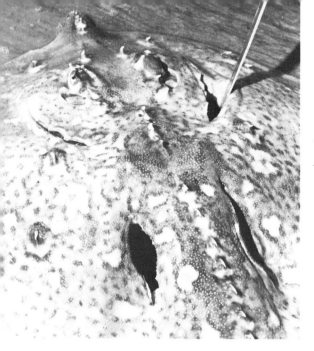

71 Cutting a thornback ray so that it bleeds. Slit through the gill openings and down the gut cavity close to each side of the backbone. Hang the fish for a few days so that the blood runs out and the skin loosens.

The worst place to keep dead fish is a sealed plastic bag exposed to sunlight. The best is a cooler box fitted with icepacks or filled with chunks of ice. Failing that, a sack dipped in the sea and then kept in the shade will suffice. Coolness, dampness and adequate ventilation are the three essentials. Mackerel and the smaller species are well preserved in a bucket of seawater. Cod and the other autumn and winter species are no problem especially at night. A good cod night is so cold that the fish freeze solid within minutes of being caught.

Many fishes are better eaten as soon as possible. Whiting straight from the sea are delicately flavoured and relatively firm, but after a day or so become soft and dull. Freezing will not preserve the texture and taste. On the other hand, cod is better after a few days in the refrigerator or freezer; the flesh hardens up into white flakes which are much easier to handle on the plate. Mackerel are never the same after storage; indeed they are at their best cooked in the open air. A stored mackerel is a dull, dreary beast totally lacking the steak-like texture of a fresh one. Rays and dogfish—in fact any of the cartilaginous species—should always be left for a few days. The flavour improves with keeping and the carcase is much easier to butcher. Peeling the skin from a fresh thornback ray is a job to give to your worst enemy. Hung from a nail on the back of the shed door—an old East Anglian custom with rays—the fish softens up in a day or so, and life is much more pleasant.

Deep freezing is one of the better ways of keeping fish. There is some controversy as to how the fish should be prepared for freezing. Some authorities recommend filleting first, others prefer to store the whole fish. Some say the fish should be washed, others say leave it in the natural slime. I have found that filleting first is more convenient because you can take out just enough for one meal. A whole fish must be thawed, cut, then eaten. Never refreeze a fish because the risk of food poisoning is high. As for washing, I find it too messy to bother with. Unwashed fish does not leak as much while hardening and seems to retain more flavour. Theoretically, the flesh will keep for several months, but after about six weeks in a normal domestic freezer some deterioration seems to take place. The thawed fish seems soggy and tasteless; sometimes it actually disintegrates in the pan.

PREPARING THE CATCH FOR THE TABLE

Flatfishes

SKINNED WHOLE FISH

Slit the belly from vent to gills and shake out the internal organs. Lay the fish right way up on a board, then nick the skin over the tail root (fig 25). Slide the blade just under the skin and loosen a flap about 2 in

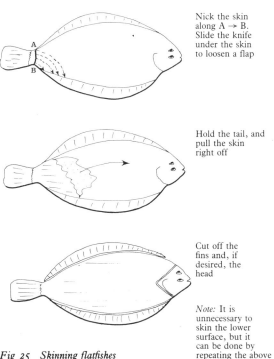

Nick the skin along A → B. Slide the knife under the skin to loosen a flap

Hold the tail, and pull the skin right off

Cut off the fins and, if desired, the head

Note: It is unnecessary to skin the lower surface, but it can be done by repeating the above

Fig 25   Skinning flatfishes

117

(5 cm) long. Hold the fish down by pressing the knife against the tail fin, grasp the loose flap and peel it back until the whole back of the fish is bared. The head may be cut off or left on according to preference; it is customary to leave on soles' heads but to cut off those of lemon soles, dabs and most other species. Trim off the main fins, tidy up any small patches of skin that still adhere, and the job is done.

FILLETING

Lay the gutted fish right way up on a board with the head towards you. Make a deep cut from the backbone to the fin in a line that follows the 'neck' (fig 26). Slide in the blade and cut along the backbone and skeleton until a flap of meat is raised. Lift the flap and slide the blade

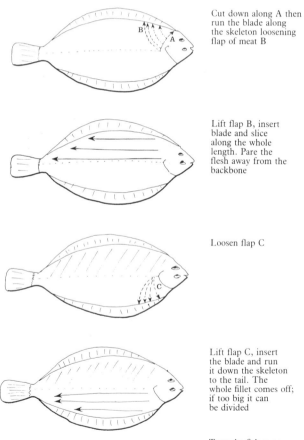

Cut down along A then run the blade along the skeleton loosening flap of meat B

Lift flap B, insert blade and slice along the whole length. Pare the flesh away from the backbone

Loosen flap C

Lift flap C, insert the blade and run it down the skeleton to the tail. The whole fillet comes off; if too big it can be divided

Turn the fish over and repeat the exercise on the lower fillet

Fig 26 Filleting flatfishes

along the skeleton from head to tail, thus freeing a half fillet. Pare it away over the backbone, press the knife through to the other fin, then cut down from head to tail. The whole fillet will now come away, leaving a quite clean backbone and skeleton. Turn the fish over and repeat the procedure to slice off the lower fillet. If necessary, divide the fillets lengthwise to make a total of four.

Small roundfishes including mackerel and whiting

These small fishes may be filleted but are better left whole or simply opened up flat. Gut and wash them, then remove the head by laying the fish on its side, lifting the pectoral fin and running the knife blade down the back of the fin root into the back of the neck. Turn the fish over and make a similar cut on the other side of the neck. Break the neck and pull off the head with a twist-and-pull action of the wrists. The vee cut into the neck is much better than a simple cross cut: more meat is obtained that way, and in many species the flesh here is of the highest quality. Then cut off the tail and trim away the fins. Whole fishes can be baked or grilled but if the body is a little too thick for efficient cooking, open the belly flaps, slit the bones and skin along the gut cavity where it joins the backbone, turn the fish over and press down firmly along the whole length of the back. The body then opens up like a kipper.

Big roundfishes

CUTLETS

Lay the fish on its side and cut off the head in the manner described for the smaller fishes. Cut the body into chunks about $1\frac{1}{2}$ in (4 cm) wide. If the fish is very tough, use a cleaver to chop through the backbone. It might help if the scales are removed before starting to cut: this is done by scraping the skin from tail to head with the back of the knife (see Plate 72). With bass and other sharp finned fishes, cut off the spiked fins beforehand because there is a great risk of running a spike into your hand so deeply that infection ensues.

FILLETS

Make the normal vee cuts into the back of the head (fig 27). Lay the fish on its side and run the knife all the way down one side of the backbone and fins. Cut down the full length of the fish gradually slicing off the meat in one slab. When the cut is deeper than the backbone, push the blade all the way through into the gut cavity, then slice down from head to tail so that the whole fillet comes away (see Plate 73). Trim off fins and loose skin. Then turn the fish over and repeat the exercise on the other fillet. Work carefully and slowly because fish are very slippery and it is all too easy to cut your hand. If you are filleting lots of cold fish, your hands may become so numbed that you do not notice the wound until blood spurts everywhere. **119**

72 *Scraping off the scales from a bass. A blunt knife or the back of a blade scraped from tail to head will strip off the scales, but watch out for the sharp spines on the fins and gill covers. It is better to cut them off first.*

73 *A complete fillet neatly removed from a cod. All roundfish can be cut this way, and waste is minimal.*

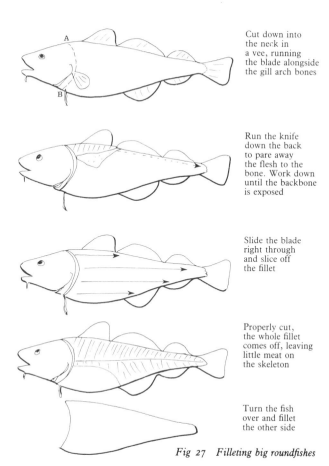

Cut down into
the neck in
a vee, running
the blade alongside
the gill arch bones

Run the knife
down the back
to pare away
the flesh to the
bone. Work down
until the backbone
is exposed

Slide the blade
right through
and slice off
the fillet

Properly cut,
the whole fillet
comes off, leaving
little meat on
the skeleton

Turn the fish
over and fillet
the other side

Fig 27   Filleting big roundfishes

RAYS

Let the fish hang several days to loosen up and bleed. Lay it face down
on a board and drive a nail through its head to hold it steady (fig 28).
Cut the leading edge of the wings right off—that is, a thin strip of skin
and gristle running from wing root to tip. Cut down between the body
and the wings so that the wings are held on by a small section in the
middle). Nick the skin in that area, and slide in the blade until a flap of
skins loosens. Pick up the skin with a pair of pliers or pincers and rip it
off the whole wing. Repeat on the other wing, then turn the ray over
and skin the lower surfaces. Cut off the wings by severing the joint
between them and the body. There is some meat on the ray's body:
along the tail section and behind the eyes. This latter meat is in the
form of two fatty lumps called 'eyeballs'. On most rays, however, the
amount and quality of meat on the main body is hardly worth the effort
of carving out.

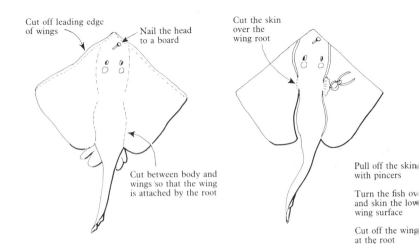

Cut off leading edge of wings

Nail the head to a board

Cut between body and wings so that the wing is attached by the root

Cut the skin over the wing root

Pull off the skin with pincers

Turn the fish over and skin the lower wing surface

Cut off the wing at the root

Fig 28   Preparing rays

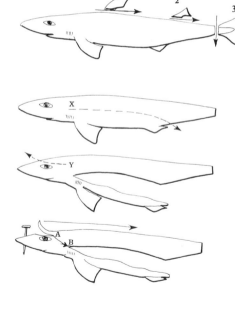

Cut off the fins 1–3

Push blade right through the fish at X then cut away the complete skin and gut cavity

Push right through at Y and cut away

Pull on the skin flap and strip off the skin to the tail. Then cut off the waste along A–B

Note: Dogfishes are tough to strip and it helps to nail the head to a board. You can then pull harder

Fig 29   Preparing dogfishes, etc.

DOGFISHES, SMOOTHOUNDS AND TOPE

Cut off the dorsal fins and the tail (fig 29). Insert the knife just above the gill slits and push it right through the body. Cut along then down at an angle so that the knife comes out just behind the pelvic fins. Make a second cut all the way through the body just forward and above the start of the first cut. Push the knife towards the head so that it comes out to leave a loose flap over the eyes. If necessary, drive a nail through the head to hold it firmly to the board, grasp the head flap and rip it towards the tail. The whole skin peels off as if it were a stocking.

Note on metrication

Metric equivalents of all significant measurements, to the nearest round figure, are given in the text. As far as casting distances, water depth and similar general measurements are concerned, this is straightforward enough.

The tackle specifications are not so simple. The metric figures given here are simply the equivalents, in metric terms, of the standard British weights, and are intended only as a guide to the nearest standard metric size for buyers of tackle in countries using the metric system.

In the next few years, Britain will eventually have to fall in line with this system. Already most lines and many lures are specified in metric because of their foreign manufacture, then changed to Imperial for the home market. Some British tackle companies already use a dual system for line breaking strain and lure weight. The conversion of rod length and sinker mass is more difficult. Straightforward application of the conversion factors is absurd: a 9 ft rod is unlikely to be advertised as 2.74 m. Sinkers of 1, 2 and 3 oz are most unlikely to become 28.35, 56.99 and 85.0 g when Britain eventually goes completely metric. Steps will be taken to phase in the new measures; otherwise production costs will be staggering. It will probably lead to a whole new set of specifications. For instance, sinkers of 30, 60, 90, 120, 150 and 180 g could replace the present 1–6 oz range. Although these are not exact equivalents, the new range would be close enough to allow the use of existing casting rods, and at the same time much easier to remember.